CHEVROLET
CHEVELLE and MONTE CARLO
1964-72

includes Malibu, 350, SS, Concours and Nomad series

James H. Moloney

Motorbooks International
Publishers & Wholesalers Inc
Osceola, Wisconsin 54020, USA ®

First published in 1986 by Motorbooks International Publishers & Wholesalers, Inc., PO Box 2, 729 Prospect Avenue, Osceola, Wisconsin 54020, USA

©James H. Moloney, 1986

Printed and bound in the United States of America

Editor William F. Kosfeld

Motorbooks International books are also available at discounts in bulk quantity for industrial or sales-promotional use. For details write to the Marketing Manager at the publisher's address.

Library of Congress Cataloging in Publication Data
Moloney, James H.

Chevrolet Chevelle and Monte Carlo, 1964-1972.
1. Chevelle automobile–History. 2. Monte Carlo automobile–History. I. Title.
TL215.C48M65 1985   629.2'222   84-29598
ISBN 0-87938-196-5 (pbk.)

PREFACE

I guess you could say I was born loving Chevrolets. Whether it was the bow-tie emblem that intrigued me on the cars when I was a kid, their logo seen at Chevrolet dealerships, the whine of a six-cylinder engine, the familiar clutch chatter or the throaty sound from a V-8, they have always been my favorite car.

I've owned twenty-six Chevies, which were not overnight cars that moved on to another owner the next morning. All have stayed with me for a good long while. Currently there are thirteen residing right here at my house. Some have been with me since they were new or owned by an immediate member of the family since new. So, when Motorbooks International asked me if I was interested in doing a book on Chevelle and Monte Carlo, I was only too eager to please, since these have always been hot items with me. They appear to be growing in popularity every month.

I wish to thank GM Photographic, Chevrolet Motor Division and those who allowed me to photograph their personal cars in order to help make this an enjoyable book for you to view. I hope it might add to your literature collection of Chevrolet memorabilia.

Jim Moloney

CONTENTS

CHAPTER ONE
Chevy Unveiled The Chevelle In Its 1964 Lineup

The Chevelle was introduced to the public on September 29, 1963. The car was well received by the public chiefly because of its size. Many people began to see the full-size Chevrolet as almost equal to Cadillac in size and performance. For those desiring a smaller car with the quality Chevrolet had been noted for, the Chevelle appeared to be the answer.

Semon E. Knudsen, General Motors vice president and general manager of Chevrolet, said Chevrolet would build five lines and forty-three models for the 1964 model run. Among them were eleven models in the Chevelle line. These included the Malibu Super Sport, Malibu and 300 series.

Chevrolet offered a two-door wagon in both the 300 series and Malibu, which was something new for the company, since the last two-door wagon was the 1960 Brookwood. The two-door wagon had a slanting rear edge on its doors reminiscent of the 1955-57 Nomad. Two six-cylinders and three V-8s were offered on the all-new, 115-inch-wheelbase car.

Prices ranged from $2,220 for the six-cylinder Chevrolet 300 two-door sedan to $2,846 for the Malibu Super Sport convertible.

The most popular model for the year was the Malibu four-door sedan, which carried a price tag of $2,338 in six-cylinder style; it brought $2,446 if the customer chose the V-8 model. The Malibu models all came with deluxe wheel covers which were not the same as the three-way spinners used on the Super Sport.

Seen here is a Malibu sedan in the once-famous Mobil Economy Run. This particular year the event left Pasadena, California, and ended in New York City. Chevrolet sponsored teenagers as a publicity feature to encourage safe driving among the country's youth.

The basic six-cylinder consisted of a 194 ci engine that developed 120 hp. The second six-cylinder engine was the 230 ci Turbo-Thrift which gave 155 hp. This optional engine had a suggested retail price of $43.05 extra. Chevrolet gave these engines chrome valve covers and other accents. For the V-8 engines, the 195 hp Turbo-Fire of 283 ci was the standard version with two-barrel carburetor and single exhaust.

In addition to this V-8 was the four-barrel, dual-exhaust 220 hp engine of the same displacement. This engine carried a manufacturer suggested retail price of $53.80 extra. The most powerful V-8s came later in the year. They were 327 ci engines, developing 250 hp with single exhaust or, equipped with larger valves and dual exhaust, 300 hp.

These mid-season engines were needed to help Chevy keep its image of offering one peppy V-8. Since Pontiac had its 389 ci V-8 option (available in the GTO), Chevrolet was crying urgently for something to let the public know the Chevelle had an engine that could hold its own with comparable intermediate muscle cars.

The available transmissions were the regular three-speed, Powerglide and overdrive for each series. A four-speed unit was available only for V-8-equipped cars. Overdrive cost $107.60 additional and was offered only with base engines; six-cylinder Powerglide cars were $188.30 more; V-8s cost $199.10. The four-speed option was $188.30 for the V-8-equipped vehicles.

Chevelle offered full coil suspension at each wheel with a built-in leveling action for exceptional handling and stability. Self-adjusting brakes were another standard feature of the big, new car, with air cooling through wheel slots to help resist fading.

Available power assists consisted of power brakes for $43.05, power steering $86.10, four-way power front seat (not available on Malibu SS models or four-speed-transmission cars) $64.60, power windows $102.25 (side windows only on Chevelle two-door 300 station wagon $59.20), power tailgate windows for six-passenger station wagons (standard on three-seat models) $26.90, power-operated convertible top $53.80.

Two types of air conditioning were available. The

A popular seller in the first year of production was the Malibu Super Sport coupe, referred to as Model 5737. It weighed 2,875 pounds and sold for $2,765 as a six-cylinder. The deluxe wheel covers were standard equipment on all Super Sport models.

This is a Chevelle 300 four-door station wagon that sold for $2,555 as a six-cylinder model and $2,663 if the customer preferred it as a V-8.

A fully equipped Malibu Super Sport convertible as shown from the 1964 Chevelle accessory catalog. The unit carried dual, rear-mounted quarter-panel antennas. The left mount, however, was classed as a dummy antenna. It sold for $7 on all coupes and convertibles. The right antenna was $8.25 as suggested by the manufacturer.

Custom DeLuxe included a 55 amp Delcotron generator and sold for $317.45. The more popular style was the Four-Season unit of heater and air conditioner combined, which cost the customer $363.70. Either type required cars with V-8 engines to use 7.00x14-inch tires.

Appearance accessories were plentiful, ranging from bumper-guard equipment for $9.70 per pair to simulated wire wheel covers at $75.35 for a set of four.

The Chevelle weighed 2,825 pounds for a 300 two-door sedan and tipped the scale at 3,240 pounds for the Malibu four-door, nine-passenger station wagon. All models came with 6.50x14 tires except for station wagons and all units equipped with air conditioning, which required 7.00x14's.

The comfortilt steering wheel was available on all models equipped with power steering and Power-glide or four-speed transmissions. It cost the buyer an additional $43.05.

Heavy-duty equipment such as 3.36:1 rear axle, 70 amp hour battery, Superlift shock absorbers and tachometer (for V-8 engines) were just a few of the options available for those whose cars were to see extra duty during their lives. This type of package was recommended for taxi and police car use.

The 1964 model run offered fifteen solid-tone colors and eleven two-tone combinations.

Models most sought after today are the SS cars with their personal touches such as special, full wheel covers; SS nameplates on the rear quarter panels; foam-cushioned front bucket seats; and unique dashboard instrumentation including ammeter, oil pressure and temperature gauges. The floor-mounted shift lever for either Powerglide or stick shift for four-speed transmission gave the feel of driving in a sports car. Special additional appointments such as the deluxe steering wheel with its chrome horn ring; deep twist carpeting; electric clock; and options (which most cars came equipped with) such as electric tachometer, positraction rear end, power steering and sintered-metallic brake linings helped make this the start of many years of popular Chevelles to follow.

The 1964 Chevelle had a production run of 328,400 units; of these, 68,300 were in the 300 series. Breaking

A dash view of the 1964 Chevelle Malibu. Shown here are the Four-Season air-conditioning ducts on the lower corners of the dashboard. The very functional instrument board includes a gas gauge and speedometer. All control knobs were recessed to decrease reflections. An electric clock and glovebox light were considered standard equipment in the Malibu and Super Sport models. A tachometer was available for an additional $39.75.

The horizontal grille bars for the 1964 Chevelle are seen here with Chevrolet spelled out in block letters at the base of the hood.

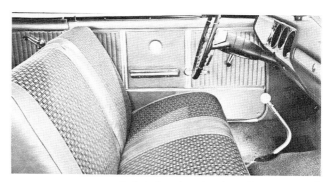

An interior view showing a floor-mounted four-speed unit in a Malibu. All Malibu and Super Sport models had carpeted floors.

it down further, 53,000 were equipped with six-cylinder engines and 15,300 were V-8 vehicles. In the Malibu series 86,900 cars came off the assembly line as six-cylinders, while the remaining 62,000 Malibus used V-8 engines. The Super Sport showed a run of 76,860 six-cylinders and V-8s combined. The wagons had 17,100 six-cylinder units produced with the remaining 26,900 coming as V-8s.

One of the noticeable differences between the Super Sport models and the regular Malibu and 300 series was the lack of mid-body-panel trim moldings which were part of the regular package on the other two series. The SS cars had their lower body edge outlined in bright metal from front wheelbase to rear bumper. Another thin, upper-body-edge outline molding added to the Super Sport's detailing.

I always had a soft spot for these first Chevelle models, chiefly because of their size and because of a personal experience. I was to take part in the 1964 Mobil Economy Run as a chaperon, you might say, to a group of teenagers who were to drive Chevelles in the event. These young people came from ten cities throughout the country where they made history as Chevrolet's Teen Team. The Mobil event began in Pasadena on April 3, 1964, and ended April 9 at the New York World's Fair. This historic occasion was the only time Chevrolet abandoned the use of experienced drivers for the economy run. Chevrolet felt this would spotlight the driving capabilities of America's youth.

Before the run actually took place, classroom navigation and instruction in highway safety were taught for several days to these youth. Then they drove locally and on short trips for approximately 6,000 miles before the big send-off early on the morning of April 3. I was teaching school at the time and, unfortunately, at the last minute our Easter recess did not coincide with the Mobil Economy Run and I wasn't able to take part. Needless to say I was extremely disappointed. In retrospect, if I had been on the trip I'm sure today I could recall every minute detail of it. Whereas, now, over twenty years later I haven't the faintest recollection of what took place in the classroom during that particular week!

This was the standard hubcap used in all 1964 Chevelles except the Super Sport models.

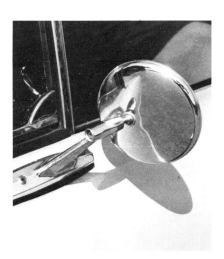

The stock-mounted door-side mirror for Chevelles in 1964.

This is the correct fender designation on all 1964 Chevelles equipped with the 230 ci six-cylinder engine.

A conservative-looking 1964 Chevelle Malibu sport coupe that sold new for $2,365 when equipped with the base six-cylinder engine.

Chevelle didn't fare all that well mileagewise but still made history seeing these young drivers as part of the Mobil Economy Run program. The top car came in with 18.75 mpg followed by 18.18 mpg and last was a sedan with 17.03 mpg.

A standard-equipped Chevelle for 1964 is seen here. Note the blank dash panel found in cars equipped without a radio, as was the case with this vehicle.

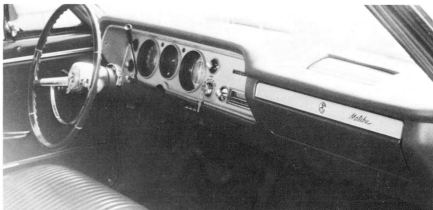

A view of the 1964 Chevelle Malibu interior. Note the nameplate mounted on the glove compartment door. This was one of the distinguishing marks to help differentiate Malibu models from the other series.

This immaculate 283 engine compartment belongs to a 1964 Chevelle convertible that is owned by Len Cormier, of Cormier Chevrolet Company in Long Beach, California.

This 1964 Chevelle wheel displays non-stock trim rings. Chevelle only used full wheel discs or simulated wire wheel covers as accessory wheel dressups for the model run. Also note the checkered flags, signifying that it has a big-block engine.

A 1964 Chevelle Malibu wagon is wearing only the basic equipment. The tailgate for the 1964 Chevelle opened downward giving room to crawl into the rear compartment to place luggage and equipment. As a six-passenger model it sold for $2,744. If the nine-passenger model was ordered it cost $2,841.

The roof luggage carrier added more usable luggage space to the station wagon. A luggage carriage cover was also available. The accessory item cost the owner an additional $43.05 in 1964.

This 1964 Chevelle Malibu wagon sports the rare window vent shades which protect from inclement weather and the sun. The "knuckle scratcher" door handles are from an earlier era of Chevrolet accessories.

Owner Gary Willson stands proudly beside his dependable 1964 Chevelle Malibu wagon. The car originally belonged to his grandfather, George Willson, of Burbank, California. The car has given many years of dependable transportation.

COLOR AND TRIM SELECTIONS

Malibu Super Sport — ALL VINYL (Super Sport Coupe / Super Sport Convertible)

Interior Trim Codes:
- A—Aqua
- B—Blue
- C—Saddle
- D—Red
- E—Black
- F—Fawn
- H—White/Aqua
- V—Optional Fawn Vinyl
- S—White/Black
- Y—Slate/Gunmetal

SOLID EXTERIOR COLORS & CODE		Fawn	White/Aqua	White/Black	Red	Blue	Saddle	Black	Slate/Gunmetal
Tuxedo Black	AA	F	H	S	D	B	C	E	Y
Ermine White	CC	F	H	S	D	B	C	E	Y
Glacier Gray	WW			S				E	Y
Madeira Maroon	NN	F		S	D		C	E	
Regal Red	RR	F		S	D			E	
Sierra Tan	SS	F					C	E	
Cameo Beige	VV	F			D		C	E	
Crocus Yellow	YY			S				E	
Willow Green	HH	F		S				E	
Cypress Green	JJ	F					C	E	
Artesian Turquoise	KK	F	H	S				E	
Tahitian Turquoise	LL	F	H						
Mist Blue	DD	F		S		B		E	
Danube Blue	EE	F				B			Y
Evening Orchid	PP			S				E	

TWO-TONE EXTERIOR COMBINATIONS & CODE
(Not available on Convertible models)

		Fawn	White/Aqua	White/Black	Red	Blue	Saddle	Black	Slate/Gunmetal
Cameo Beige/Madeira Maroon	VN	F							
Sierra Tan/Cameo Beige	SV	F					C		
Cypress Green/Cameo Beige	JV	F					C		
Mist Blue/Ermine White	DC					B			
Crocus Yellow/Ermine White	YC			S				E	
Ermine White/Artesian Turq	CK		H						
Tahitian Turq/Artesian Turq	LX		H						
Glacier Gray/Tuxedo Black	WA							E	Y

COLOR AND TRIM SELECTIONS

	Malibu — CLOTH & VINYL (Sport Coupe & Sedan) / ALL VINYL (Convertible, Station Wagon)					300 Deluxe — CLOTH & VINYL (Sedans, Station Wagons)			Chevelle 300 — CLOTH & VINYL (Sedans) / ALL VINYL (Station Wagon)			Fawn Vinyl Optional—Sedans
	Fawn	Aqua	Red	Blue	Saddle	Fawn	Aqua	Red	Fawn	Aqua	Red	
Tuxedo Black	F	A	D	B	C	F	A	D	F	A	D	V
Ermine White	F	A	D	B	C	F	A	D	F	A	D	V
Glacier Gray												
Madeira Maroon	F		D		C	F		D	F		D	V
Regal Red	F		D			F		D	F		D	V
Sierra Tan	F				C	F			F			V
Cameo Beige	F		D		C	F		D	F		D	V
Crocus Yellow												
Willow Green	F					F			F			V
Cypress Green	F				C	F			F			V
Artesian Turquoise	F	A				F	A		F	A		V
Tahitian Turquoise	F	A				F	A		F	A		V
Mist Blue	F			B		F			F			V
Danube Blue	F			B		F			F			V
Evening Orchid												

	Fawn	Aqua	Red	Blue	Saddle	Fawn	Aqua	Red	Fawn	Aqua	Red	
Cameo Beige/Madeira Maroon	F					F			F			V
Sierra Tan/Cameo Beige	F				C	F			F			V
Cypress Green/Cameo Beige	F				C	F			F			V
Mist Blue/Ermine White				B								
Crocus Yellow/Ermine White												
Ermine White/Artesian Turq		A					A			A		
Tahitian Turq/Artesian Turq		A					A			A		
Glacier Gray/Tuxedo Black												

Color and trim selections for 1964.

CHAPTER TWO
Chevelles Get More Powerful

Chevelle entered the automotive market in 1965 with pretty much the same appearance package as it had in 1964. This year saw some new models introduced to the line while others were phased out of production. The 300 series now offered a 300 DeLuxe which came as a two-door sedan, four-door sedan, and four-door two-seat wagon. Prices for this new series ranged from $2,339 to $2,674 in V-8 models. Chevelle did not offer a three-seat wagon for 1965. The 300 DeLuxe convertible was cataloged but from the research I have done on this model it appears it was never produced. Prices ranged from $2,156 for the two-door six-cylinder 300 sedan to $3,035 for the Malibu Super Sport V-8 convertible. The 1965 Chevelle grew in length to 196 inches for all models but wagons, which were increased to 201.4 inches overall.

The same engine teams were available as in the previous year. The 120 hp six was unchanged as the base six-cylinder engine, while the optional 230 ci six was down-rated to 140 hp and lost its chrome touches. The 300 hp 327 ci V-8 that came in late 1964 cars was now more plentiful. The 327 V-8 was available only

This fisherman is enjoying the easy life beside his 1965 Malibu four-door station wagon. This was Chevelle's highest-priced wagon for 1965. As a six-cylinder it sold for $2,647 but if the V-8 engine was ordered the car sold for $2,755. The weight of the Malibu wagon was 3,225 pounds as a six-cylinder and 3,355 pounds as a V-8.

A popular model with those who enjoyed the open air was the 1965 "rag-top" Malibu convertible. The car was available as a six-cylinder for $2,583 or as a V-8 for $2,698.

with four-speed or Powerglide transmissions. Both 250 and 300 hp versions used a 3.31:1 standard rear axle ratio.

"Big-block" power was soon to appear beneath Chevelle hoods, but before it did, the "small-block" 327 was released in a stunning 350 hp version that ruled the streets briefly: RPO L 79. Popping the hood on a car so equipped revealed a dual-snorkel chrome-plated air cleaner. Beneath it was an aluminum manifold and four-barrel carburetor designed to feed the 11.01:1 port heads ample quantities of premium fuel. The 350 hp 327—Chevrolet called it "the perfect squelch" in ads—was found in few 1965 Chevelles, many of them standard Malibu. It was a serious racer's engine, and called for heavy-duty suspension.

Late in the season came a 396 engine rated at 375 hp with hydraulic valve lifters, four-barrel carburetor and dual exhausts. This engine represented a completely new design.

With all the mid- and late-season offerings from other manufacturers, Chevrolet felt it had to be part of the act too. One of its big surprises, and a model really sought after today by Chevrolet enthusiasts, was the extremely late Z-16 Chevelle. It came with a long list of extra-cost options which were part of the regular package. These options included the 160 mph speedometer, a high-rpm tach and the new Corvette 396 big-block, slightly civilized with a hydraulic cam to give 375 hp. A four-speed gearbox was advised for the 375 hp unit.

Roughly 200 of these screaming machines were produced. They were available only as hardtop coupe models. The Z-16 Chevelle had a curb weight of 3,650 pounds and cost $1,501.05 more than the comparable Malibu Super Sport coupe.

It was originally intended to sell the Z-16 only to the top Chevrolet dealers in the country, with a maximum of one per dealer! Whether these plans were carried out I am not sure, nor does anyone of Chevrolet knowledge seem to know today. These machines could do 0-60 in 6.5 seconds and a quarter mile in 14.9 seconds. Needless to say, they held their own on any race circuit.

A young kid in our neighborhood was given one of

This factory photo shows one view of the 1965.

For an extra dress-up look, Chevelle offered this deluxe stainless wheel disc for $15.95 for a set of four (part number 986079). The Super Sport came with its own special wheel covers as standard equipment.

Wire wheel covers also were available in each series of Chevelle for 1965. They sold for $58.95 per set of four. The part number was 985699.

A close-up view of Chevelle's new grille, massive deep-section front bumper and the grille emblem.

14

these Super Sports with the 396 engine. He took it out the first night to impress everyone—including his girlfriend—and in the process, with his foot in the carburetor, tried to make a quick turn in a cul-de-sac. He didn't make the turn he had hoped for and the five-hour-old luster-black beauty hit some fairly well rooted trees and then a retaining wall to make a near-totaled-out wreck of this car. Fortunately, he came out of the incident with only minor bruises. The boy's father felt the best way to get out of it without a full police investigation was to just say the throttle stuck! Only problem was, too many people had seen him leave the driveway and knew his driving record. These are the kind of people who have ruined the muscle car image and made a bad name for other young people who enjoy these cars and are responsible.

Quick identification marks to distinguish the three series were easily seen on the side panels: The 300 series simply stated Chevelle 300 on the rear quarter panels. The 300 Deluxe carried a chrome molding on its lower beltline. The Malibu had a trim molding at the middle of the beltline where it does its practical job in parking lots. Again this year (as in 1964) Super Sports featured stainless-steel, fender-opening cutouts and special wheel covers with the SS identification in the center of the hub; the front appearance quickly told Chevelle fans it was a Super Sport by its black accents in the grille area. At the rear, the base of the trunk was surrounded by black highlights with the SS emblem neatly placed on the right next to the taillamp.

The tire size for 1965 basic models was 6.95x14. For all cars equipped with air conditioning or 327 ci engines, 7.35x14 tires were required.

New for 1965 was the use of the black vinyl tops seen only on the sport coupe models with a solid exterior color. The vinyl roof cost $75.35 extra.

For 1965, Chevelle came in fifteen solid colors and eight two-tone combinations.

Chevelle coupe to be SS model. Just a quick look will tell you these are views of the popular Malibu coupe. The rear quarter panels designate it as a Malibu Chevelle rather than a Super Sport; bodyside trim, plain wheel covers and lack of the deck designation denote it as a Super Sport. This particular unit also carries the 327 checkered flags on the front fenders telling you it sold for $3,175 with the V-8 engine. Some of the standard equipment on this model include carpeting, glovebox light, clock, door armrests, and front and rear ashtrays. This proved to be the most popular model in the Malibu line.

The Chevelle model numbers were as follows for 1965:

Six-Cylinder Models
Chevelle 300 2-door sedan   13111
Chevelle 300 4-door sedan   13169
Chevelle 300 2-door, 2-seat station wagon   13115
Chevelle 300 DeLuxe 2-door sedan   13311
Chevelle 300 DeLuxe 4-door sedan   13369
Chevelle 300 DeLuxe 4-door, 2-seat station wagon   13335
Malibu 4-door sedan   13569
Malibu sport coupe   13537
Malibu convertible   13567
Malibu station wagon   13535
Malibu Super Sport coupe   13737
Malibu Super Sport convertible   13767

V-8 Models
Chevelle 300 2-door sedan   13211
Chevelle 300 4-door sedan   13269
Chevelle 300 2-door, 2-seat station wagon   13215
Chevelle 300 DeLuxe 2-door sedan   13411
Chevelle 300 DeLuxe 4-door sedan   13469
Chevelle 300 DeLuxe 4-door, 2-seat station wagon   13435
Malibu 4-door sedan   13669
Malibu sport coupe   13637
Malibu convertible   13667
Malibu 4-door, 2-seat station wagon   13635
Malibu Super Sport convertible   13867

Production figures for Chevelle rose to 344,100 in 1965. The 300 series accounted for 31,600. Of these, 26,500 came with six-cylinder engines. The remaining 5,100 saw a V-8 powerplant. The new 300 DeLuxe models had 41,600 produced; of that total, 9,600 were V-8s. The popular Malibus totaled 152,200; of that number, 95,800 came with a V-8, leaving 56,400 as six-cylinder models. The Malibu Super Sport accounted for 81,100 units, with 72,500 carrying the V-8 block under the hood. As for station wagons, 37,600 carried the Chevelle nameplate; of those, 13,800 were six-cylinder models and 23,800 were registered as V-8s.

Chevelle's trunk loading area consisted of 27.3 cubic feet of space. In the Chevelle 300 DeLuxe, Malibu and Malibu Super Sport models the luggage compartment floor was covered for added protection.

New window and door regulators graced every Chevelle for 1965. The all-vinyl seats in the Super Sport, Malibu Convertible, Malibu and Chevelle 300 wagons can be cleaned very easily. All Malibu and Super Sport models carried a deep twist carpeting while the Chevelle 300 DeLuxe used a vinyl-coated, color-keyed rubber mat throughout. The Chevelle 300 used a durable, black-rubber floor mat.

Chevelle used this attractive instrument panel, which included deeper shrouds for the instruments, to eliminate reflections on the windshield. All models carried a color-keyed steering wheel that gave an appearance of luxury.

A view of the left rear quarter panel showing the Malibu Super Sport emblem that was used for 1965 models.

The Chevelle Malibu Super Sport coupe, Model 13737, delivered as a six, sold for $2,539. In V-8 style it carried the model number 13837 and sold for $2,647. Its distinguishing features were stainless-steel wheel cutouts, lower rear-quarter-panel identifying trim and special wheel covers with SS emblems in the center disc.

Chevelles for the second year were put to use by local police departments and taxi companies. Seen here is a 300 four-door sedan used for policework; the V-8s of 327 and 409 ci displacement were often used. Generally the six-cylinder 140 hp Turbo-Thrift of 230 ci displacement was recommended for fleet or taxi use. The 300 model in four-door use as shown sold for $2,193 as a six, and for $2,377 in V-8 style.

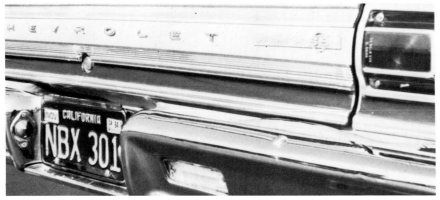

The deck designation of SS in the lower right corner was a distinguishing item seen on all of these models. This 1965 unit shows its back-up lamps placed within the bumper rather than in the taillamp assembly as was seen on the 1964 cars.

Factory-equipped stock wheel covers that were used on all Malibu Super Sports for 1965.

COLOR AND TRIM SELECTIONS

Super Sport

RPO NO. SOLID COLORS		Fawn	Aqua	Red	Blue	Saddle	Black	White (a)
	RPO NO.	770	712	706	741	710	716	730
900	Tuxedo Black	•	•	•	•	•	•	•
906	Meadow Green*	•						
908	Bahama Green*	•			•			
912	Silver Blue*				•	•		
916	Daytona Blue*				•			
918	Azure Aqua*		•			•		
919	Lagoon Aqua*		•					
920	Almond Fawn*	•			•	•		
922	Ember Red	•		•			•	•
932	Saddle Tan*	•			•			
936	Ermine White	•	•	•	•	•	•	
938	Desert Beige	•		•	•			
940	Satin Silver*		•	•	•	•		
942	Goldwood Yellow					•		
948	Palomar Red*	•		•			•	•

TWO-TONE COMBINATIONS (Not available on Convertibles)

	Upper Lower							
952	Bahama Green* & Meadow Green*						•	
954	Ermine White & Meadow Green*						•	
958	Ermine White & Silver Blue*				•			
960	Daytona Blue* & Silver Blue*				•			
962	Ermine White & Lagoon Aqua*		•					
971	Desert Beige & Saddle Tan*	•			•			
975	Desert Beige & Ember Red	•		•			•	•
982	Daytona Blue* & Satin Silver*			•	•			
988	Azure Aqua* & Ermine White		•					
993	Desert Beige & Palomar Red*	•		•			•	
996	Satin Silver* & Palomar Red*			•			•	•

*Metallic   Note. Malibu body side molding accent area Black with all body colors including two-tone.

(a) White interior with Red instrument panel, steering wheel, and carpeting.

COLOR AND TRIM SELECTIONS

Malibu / Chevelle 300

		Fawn	Aqua	Red	Blue	Saddle	Fawn (d)	Aqua	Red	Blue
	RPO NO.	742 750 (b)	748 751 (b)	771 774 (b)	730 743 (b)	767 795 (b)	743	749	770	730
900	Tuxedo Black	•	•	•	•	•	•	•	•	
906	Meadow Green*	•								
908	Bahama Green*	•				(b)	•			
912	Silver Blue*				•					•
916	Daytona Blue*				•					•
918	Azure Aqua*		•					•		
919	Lagoon Aqua*		•					•		
920	Almond Fawn*	•			•		•			
922	Ember Red	•		•			•		•	
932	Saddle Tan*	•			•		•			
936	Ermine White	•	•	•	•	•	•	•	•	•
938	Desert Beige	•	•		•		•		•	
940	Satin Silver*		•	•	•		•		•	
948	Palomar Red*	(b)	•							

952		•			•					
954		•			•					
958				•						•
960				•						
962			•					•		
971		•			•					
975		(c)	•		•			•		
982				•						•
988			•					•		
993		•		(c)		•		•		
996									•	

(b) All-vinyl—Convertible and Station Wagons only.

(c) All-vinyl—Station Wagons only.

(d) All-vinyl Fawn interior (RPO 759) available on Sedans and 4-Door Station Wagon models.

Color and trim selections for 1965.

CHAPTER THREE
Chevelles Provide Real Variety

Chevrolet offered real variety for the buyer when it introduced the 1966 line-up of twelve Chevelle models. New for the season was a swank-looking four-door hardtop sedan. I remember when I saw it introduced at our local Chevrolet dealer on October 7, 1965; I thought it was the Caprice at first. It offered a look of real quality. The popular Super Sport became more of an engine/appearance option this year with a 396 V-8 included, while bucket seats became an additional option. The overall length of the Chevelle remained 197 inches with a seventy-five-inch width and height range from 51.9 to fifty-three inches.

For powerplants, the customer had a choice of two six-cylinder engines and five V-8s. The horsepower ranged from the 120 hp six for grandma to the 396 ci V-8 which developed 325 hp or 360 hp for the muscle car fan. This 396 ci engine for 1966 saw approximately 120 cars built for public sale using the 375 hp version with the four-speed tranny. Other than these, the remaining SS 396 Chevelles produced for the year came with 325 or 360 hp engines as stated above. These engines used small-port heads and a standard

A very conservative but well-designed car was the 1966 Malibu four-door sedan. This unit sold for $2,352 as a six, and $2,458 as a V-8.

Chevelle's lowest-priced car for 1966 was this six-cylinder 300 two-door sedan, which sold for $2,165. The four-door sold for $2,202.

exhaust manifold which kept the Chevelle more in line with the remainder of General Motors' street machines for 1966.

The 1966 hardtop models had a curb weight of 3,800 pounds and could do 0-60 in 7.9 seconds. A quarter-mile run took just 15.5 seconds hitting 99 mph.

Motion Performance built a small run of 396 and 427 solid-lifter, four-speed Super Sports for 1966 with the cowl induction as used on the NASCAR (National Association for Stock Car Racing) cars. When tuned properly the 396 with special cam and a Holley four-barrel had outstanding "breathing" characteristics.

The model designation of Super Sport was changed somewhat in 1966 to Super Sport 396 and was available again (as in 1965) only in the sport coupe and convertible as the SS.

The basic 396 ci engine developed 325 hp and, like the 360 hp version, featured a four-barrel carburetor, chromed rocker covers, air cleaner cover and oil filter cap as standard equipment. Cast-aluminum pistons with a close-bore fit provided quiet operation and outstanding oil and compression control. A 10.25:1 compression ratio and special camshaft were available only on this model. Premium fuel was recommended for the engine. Simulated air scoops on the hood emphasized that a new 396 engine was standard on the SS 396 convertible and the companion sport coupe.

The 327 was offered in all but SS 396 cars. Still available, but rarely seen, was the 350 hp version. Only the 375 hp big-block 396 could compare.

The standard tire sizes on 1966 Chevelles were as follows: 7.75x14 on Super Sport 396 and wagon;

Since Chevelle dropped its two-door wagon in 1965 this 300 DeLuxe now was ranked as the lowest-priced wagon in the 1966 Chevelle line-up. As a six-cylinder it sold for $2,575, and as a V-8 for $2,681.

A little more dolled-up than the regular Malibu convertible is this SS 396 version with its wide rocker moldings and hood air scoops (also standard on the sport coupe). It came only as a V-8 and was the most expensive model for 1966 with a base price of $2,984.

7.35x14 on Malibu sport sedan with V-8 engine, convertible, and cars with a 275 hp V-8 engine; 6.95x14 on all other models.

Six-Cylinder Models

The Chevelle model numbers for 1966 were as follows:
Chevelle 300 2-door sedan   13111
Chevelle 300 4-door sedan   13169
Chevelle 300 DeLuxe 2-door sedan   13311
Chevelle 300 DeLuxe 4-door sedan   13369
Chevelle 300 DeLuxe 4-door, 2-seat station wagon   13335
(Chevelle 300 offered only two models. Gone was the 2-door, 2-seat station wagon.)
Malibu 4-door sedan   13569
Malibu sport sedan   13569
Malibu sport coupe   13517
Malibu convertible   13567
Malibu 4-door, 2-seat station wagon   13535

V-8 Models

Chevelle 300 2-door sedan   13211
Chevelle 300 4-door sedan   13269
Chevelle 300 DeLuxe 2-door sedan   13411
Chevelle 300 DeLuxe 4-door sedan   13469
Chevelle 300 DeLuxe 4-door, 2-seat station wagon   13435
Malibu 4-door sedan   13669
Malibu 4-door sport sedan   13639
Malibu sport coupe   13617
Malibu convertible   13667
Malibu 4-door, 2-seat station wagon   13635
SS 396 sport coupe   13817
SS 396 convertible   13867

Redesigned body panels and a front end with wrap-around grille gave the car a long and low silhouette. The rooflines also were new for two- and four-door sedans. The hardtops came with a new roofline too, employing wide, flowing rear quarters and a recessed rear window.

The production run for Chevelle in 1966 amounted to 412,000 units. Of this production 28,600 came from the 300 series with 5,300 using the V-8 engines. The 300 DeLuxe series produced 37,600 vehicles, including 10,500 V-8s. The Malibu series had 241,800 units, including 189,300 V-8s. The popular SS 396 cars accounted for 72,300, all were V-8s. The wagon production amounted to 31,900 and of this figure 23,000 used the V-8 block.

An interior shot of the Malibu for 1966. Deep twist carpeting, patterned cloth-and-vinyl seats backed by foam cushioning and vinyl sidewalls made for a rather deluxe interior.

Well-balanced lines were quite evident in the newest model for 1966. This is Model 13639. In other words, it's a Malibu V-8 sport sedan that displays its antenna on the right rear quarter panel. The antenna also could be placed on the front right cowl. This unit sold for $2,564.

The SS 396 coupe's all-vinyl interior with Strato-bucket seats came in a variety of colors for the customer to choose from.

A fully synchronized four-speed as shown here was meant for those with the muscle car mania.

This is another view of the 1966 Malibu sport sedan. The absence of the pillars made this a very popular model for the year. This unit is equipped with radio, side mirror, whitewall tires and the full-cover wheel discs that added to an already sharp-looking car.

TISSUE DISPENSERS AND LITTER CONTAINERS

For instrument panel mounting
Handy dispensers and litter containers for all model Chevelles.

SPEED AND CRUISE CONTROL

"YOUR AUTOMATIC PILOT"

An electronic robot that warns you when you have reached a preset speed on the speed control wheel.

FEATURES increased gasoline economy, relief from driving tension and speedometer watching.

TRAILER HITCH

An ideal hitch for light utility or boat trailers, will handle a 2000 pound load with a 200 pound vertical tongue load.

INSIDE REAR VIEW NON-GLARE MIRROR

DAY TIME

NIGHT TIME

A wide angle prismatic mirror that can be changed from clear to non-glare for safer night driving.

WINDSHIELD WASHER

Electrically operated washer that starts the wiper and pump when the button is depressed.

AUTOMATIC TRUNK OPENER

A control valve located in the glove compartment automatically opens the trunk lid.

SPARE TIRE AND WHEEL COVER

A heavy vinyl cover made from matching color and material used to line trunk interior.

REAR DECK LID LUGGAGE CARRIER

Adds additional cargo capacity and can be easily adapted to many type deck lid ski racks.

7

VENTSHADES

Helps prevent window fogging on rainy days by providing additional ventilation.

REAR VIEW MIRROR

The mirror glass is chrome coated to prevent fogging and discoloring of the glass.

AUTO COMPASS

A dependable compass that attaches to the windshield glass. Compass dial is lighted by a battery that can be incorporated in the compass.

ASH TRAY LAMP

Lights the ash tray interior when headlamps are turned on at night.

UNDERHOOD LAMP

Lights the entire engine compartment automatically when hood is opened.

GLOVE COMPARTMENT LAMP

Automatically lights glove compartment area when the door is opened.

LUGGAGE COMPARTMENT LAMP

Lights the entire luggage area when trunk is opened.

ELECTRIC CLOCKS

Two clocks are available one for the instrument cluster, one for top instrument panel mounting.

HAND PORTABLE SPOT LAMP

Works in any 12 volt cigarette lighter.

A wide variety of custom accessories were available for the 1966 Chevelle buyer as shown here from a 1966 accessory catalog.

The checkered flags denoting the 396 ci engine were displayed on the lower front fender of this 1966 Chevelle.

A mint 1966 Chevelle Super Sport with the 396 ci engine that developed 325 hp. This unit technically was called Model 13817 and carried a base sticker price of $2,776.

Classed as a model by itself was the new SS 396 Malibu sport coupe. Red-striped tires were considered the "in" thing at the time and the SS 396 came equipped with them. This unit could be delivered from your local dealer for $2,776. The vehicle weighed in at 3,375 pounds.

This is a 1966 Malibu convertible, available as a six-cylinder, Model 13567, selling for $2,588. In V-8 form it was Model 13667 and carried a price of $2,693.

The hood vents on this 1966 Chevelle were part of the standard trim package for all SS 396 cars.

A rear view of one neat 1966 Chevelle Super Sport. The SS emblems with the 396 designation encased in the panel beneath the deck lid helped to distinguish it from regular coupes. The exhaust tips on this vehicle were not stock Chevrolet accessory items.

An interior view of a 1966 Super Sport with "four-on-the-floor" and bucket seats. The dice were not a Chevrolet option.

A front view of a 1966 SS 396. Note the blacked-out grille which was part of the regular SS 396 package, and the emblem neatly arranged in the center.

A well-kept 396 ci engine is displayed under the hood of this 1966 Super Sport. The air cleaner decal tells us it's a Turbo-Jet 325 hp unit. The chrome valve covers and air cleaner were standard equipment.

This 1966 Chevelle Malibu sport coupe was less splashy than its SS 396 counterpart but also carried a price tag nearly $300 less. It sold for $2,484. The vehicle weighed 3,075 pounds. The horizontal grille bars make it easy to distinguish from the 1967 models.

Description	Opt No.	Mfr's Suggested Retail	State & Local Taxes	Total
Air Conditioning, Four-Season — Heater and air conditioner combined. Includes Heavy-Duty Radiator, Temperature-Controlled Fan, and 61-ampere Delcotron Generator. 7.35 x 14 or larger tires required on 6-cylinder Sport Sedan and V8 models	C60	$356.00		
Air Deflector, Rear Window — For Station Wagon models	C51	19.00		
Antenna, Rear — Not available with AM-FM Radio or Station Wagon models				
Power	U75	28.45		
Manual	U73	9.50		
Axles, Rear:				
3.36:1 — Available with either 6-cyl and 3-Speed (except Wagons), and 195-hp or 220-hp with 3- or 4-Speed	G76	2.15		
3.31:1 — Available with 360-hp	G94	2.15		
3.55:1 — Available with 325-hp and 360-hp	G96	2.15		
3.73:1 — Available with 325-hp	H05	N.C.		
Axle, Positraction Rear — Available in same ratios as standard axles plus 4.10:1 (325-hp and 360-hp), 4.56:1 and 4.88:1 (360-hp)	G80	36.90		
Battery, Heavy-Duty — 70-ampere-hour	T60	7.40		
Brake Linings, Sintered-Metallic	J65	36.90		
Brakes, Power	J50	42.15		
Carrier, Luggage — Station Wagons only	V55	42.15		
Clutch, Heavy-Duty — 11" clutch for standard 6-cylinder engine only. Included with Air Conditioning option. Not available with GM Air Injection Reactor	M01	5.30		
Console — Includes floor-mounted transmission control. Available only when bucket seats and 4-Speed or Powerglide (also 3-Speed on SS 396) are ordered	D55	47.40		
Convenience Equipment — Includes inside day-night mirror, outside remote-control mirror, door edge guards, luggage compartment lamp (except Wagons) and underhood lamp.				
SS 396 and Malibu				
Sport Coupes and Convertibles	Z19	21.10		
Sedans	Z19	24.25		
Station Wagons	Z19	22.15		
300 Deluxe and 300 (Also glove box lamp)				
2-Door Sedans	Z19	23.20		
4-Door Sedans	Z19	26.35		
Station Wagons	Z19	24.25		
Cooler, Transmission Oil — Available with standard 6-cylinder engine and Powerglide. Includes Heavy-Duty Radiator	M55	15.80		
Defroster, Rear Window — Available only on Sedans and Sport Coupes	C50	21.10		
Engines (Replacing standard 120-hp Hi-Thrift 194 6-cyl engine)				
140-hp Turbo-Thrift 230 — (6)	L26	26.35		
(Replacing standard 195-hp Turbo-Fire 283 V8 engine)				
220-hp Turbo-Fire 283 — (V8). Includes dual exhaust system	L77	52.70		
275-hp Turbo-Fire 327 — (V8). Includes 7.35 x 14 tires on models where equivalent or larger tires are not included (Replacing 325-hp Turbo-Jet 396 V8 engines on Super Sport 396)	L30	92.70		
360-hp Turbo-Jet 396 — (V8). Includes dual exhaust system	L34	105.35		
Engine Ventilation, Closed Positive-Type Included with 360-hp V8	K24	5.25		
Exhaust, Dual — 275-hp V8 engine	N10	$ 21.10		
Fan, Temperature-Controlled — For V8 engine only. Included with Air Conditioning	K02	15.80		
Generator, Delcotron:				
12-42-Ampere — Included with Full-Transistor Ignition. Not available with Air Conditioning	K79	10.55		
5-61-Ampere — Included with Air Conditioning	K76	21.10		
23-62-Ampere — Not available with Power Steering on 6-cylinder models or with GM Air Injection Reactor				
With Air Conditioning	K81	63.20		
Without Air Conditioning	K81	73.75		
Glass, Soft-Ray Tinted — All windows	A01	30.55		
Windshield only	A02	19.50		
GM Air Injection Reactor — Requires Closed Positive Ventilation. California registered vehicles only	K19	44.75		
Guards, Front Bumper — All models	V31	9.50		
Guards, Rear Bumper — Except Station Wagons	V32	9.50		
Harness, Shoulder — Driver and passenger. Requires Custom Deluxe Seat Belts	A85	26.35		
Headrests, Strato-Ease — Front seat only				
With optional Strato-back seats	A81	52.70		
With standard full-width seats	A82	42.15		
Heater and Defroster Deletion — Credit option. Not available with Air Conditioning	C48	70.70CR		
Horn, Tri-Volume — Except Chevelle 300 models	U03	13.70		
Ignition System, Full-Transistor — Includes 42-ampere Delcotron. For 360-hp V8 engine only	K66	73.75		
Instrumentation, Special — Available on Sport Coupes and Convertibles. Includes ammeter, temperature and oil pressure gauges, and parking brake warning light. Also includes Tachometer on V8 models				
With V8 engine	U14	79.00		
With 6-cylinder engine	U14	31.60		
Lock, Spare Wheel	P19	5.30		
Radiator, Heavy-Duty — Included with Air Conditioning or Transmission Oil Cooler	V01	10.55		
Radios, Pushbutton — With front antenna				
AM-FM Radio	U69	133.80		
AM-FM Radio and Rear Seat Speaker	U69/U80	147.00		
AM Radio	U63	57.40		
AM Radio and Rear Seat Speaker	U63/U80	70.60		
Roof Cover, Vinyl — Sport Coupe models only. Black or beige vinyl with any solid exterior color	C08	73.75		
Seat Belts — Custom Deluxe (color-matched) Front and rear, with front retractors	A39	10.55		
Seat, Power 4-Way — Available for driver's seat on bucket seat models	A46	69.55		
Seat, Power 4-Way — For conventional front seats. Not available on Chevelle 300, or models with 4-Speed transmission or bucket seats	A41	69.55		
Seats, Strato-Bucket — Available on Sport Coupe and Convertible models	A51	110.60		
Shock Absorbers, Superlift Air-Adjustable Rear only	G66	36.90		
Steering, Power	N40	$84.30		
Steering Wheel, Comfortilt — Seven positions. Available on models with Powerglide or 4-Speed transmission	N33	42.15		
Steering Wheel, Sports-Styled	N34	31.60		
Suspension, Special Front and Rear				
Station Wagon models: special front and rear springs	F40	3.70		
Other models: special front and rear springs and shock absorbers	F40	4.75		
Tachometer — With V8 engines only	U16	47.40		
Tires:				
Note: 7.75 x 14 standard on Super Sport 396 and Station Wagons. 7.35 x 14 standard on Malibu Sport Sedan with V8 engine, Convertibles and included with 275-hp V8 engine. 6.95 x 14 standard on other models. For additional tire information see page 34.				
Replacing 6.95 x 14 2-ply (4-ply rating) Blackwall, Highway Rayon Tubeless Tires				
6.95 x 14 2-ply (4-ply rating) Whitewall Rayon	P67	28.20		
7.35 x 14 2-ply (4-ply rating) Blackwall Rayon	P57	7.80		
7.35 x 14 2-ply (4-ply rating) Whitewall Rayon	P58	39.15		
7.75 x 14 2-ply (4-ply rating) Blackwall Rayon	P65	22.30		
7.75 x 14 2-ply (4-ply rating) Whitewall Rayon	P62	53.60		
7.75 x 14 4-ply (4-ply rating) Blackwall Nylon	P60	39.05		
7.75 x 14 4-ply (4-ply rating) Whitewall Nylon	P61	72.40		
Replacing 7.35 x 14 2-ply (4-ply rating) Blackwall, Highway Rayon Tubeless Tires				
7.35 x 14 2-ply (4-ply rating) Whitewall Rayon	P58	31.35		
7.75 x 14 2-ply (4-ply rating) Blackwall Rayon	P65	14.50		
7.75 x 14 2-ply (4-ply rating) Whitewall Rayon	P62	45.80		
7.75 x 14 4-ply (4-ply rating) Blackwall Nylon	P60	31.25		
7.75 x 14 4-ply (4-ply rating) Whitewall Nylon	P61	64.60		
Replacing 7.75 x 14 2-ply (4-ply rating) Blackwall, Highway Rayon Tubeless Tires				
7.75 x 14 2-ply (4-ply rating) Whitewall Rayon	P62	31.30		
7.75 x 14 4-ply (4-ply rating) Blackwall Nylon	P60	16.75		
7.75 x 14 4-ply (4-ply rating) Whitewall Nylon	P61	50.10		
▪ 7.75 x 14 4-ply (8-ply rating) Blackwall Rayon	T14	45.75		
Replacing 7.75 x 14 2-ply (4-ply rating) Red Stripe Sidewall, Special Nylon Tubeless Tires on SS 396 Models				
7.75 x 14 2-ply (4-ply rating) Whitewall Special Nylon	T07	N.C.		
Top, Convertible — Choice of white, black, or beige. See Sales Album, Colors and Fabrics section	C05	N.C.		
Top, Power-Operated Convertible	C05/C06	52.70		
Traffic Hazard Warning System	V74	11.60		
Transmissions:				
Powerglide				
With 6-cylinder engines	M35	184.35		
With 195-hp, 220-hp and 275-hp	M35	194.85		
With 325-hp and 360-hp	M35	115.90		
4-Speed Fully Synchronized — (Close-Ratio) Available with 360-hp V8	M21	105.35		
4-Speed Fully Synchronized — (Wide-Range).				
With 195-hp, 220-hp and 275-hp	M20	184.35		
With 325-hp and 360-hp	M20	105.35		
Overdrive — Available with both 6-cylinder engines, plus 195-hp and 220-hp V8's	M10	115.90		
Trim, Black Vinyl Interior — Malibu Sport Coupe and Sport Sedan only	761	10.55		
Trim, Fawn Vinyl Interior — Available on Chevelle 300 Sedans	720	5.30		
Two-Tone Finish — See Color Chart, pages 12-13, for availability		15.80		
Wheel Covers — Set of four	P01	21.10		
Wheel Covers, Mag-Style — Set of four	N96	73.75		
Wheel Covers, Simulated Wire — Set of four	P02	73.75		
Windows, Power — SS 396 and Malibu only	A31	100.10		
Window, Power Tailgate — Station Wagons	A33	26.35		

▪—Available only on Station Wagons

1966 factory-installed optional equipment.

POWER TEAMS

Engine	3-Speed Fully Synch.	Overdrive	4-Speed Fully Synch.	Powerglide
Standard 6 120-hp Hi-Thrift 194 (194-cu-in 6)	Standard	RPO M10		RPO M35
RPO L26 140-hp Turbo-Thrift 230 (230-cu-in 6)	Standard	RPO M10		RPO M35
Standard V8 195-hp Turbo-Fire 283 (283-cu-in V8)	Standard	RPO M10	RPO M20	RPO M35
RPO L77 220-hp Turbo-Fire 283 (283-cu-in V8)	Standard	RPO M10	RPO M20	RPO M35
RPO L30 275-hp Turbo-Fire 327 (327-cu-in V8)	Standard		RPO M20	RPO M35
Standard SS 396 325-hp Turbo-Jet 396 (396-cu-in V8)	Standard		RPO M20	RPO M35
RPO L34 360-hp Turbo-Jet 396 (396-cu-in V8)	Standard		RPO M20 or M21	RPO M35

Power teams for 1966.

Wheelbase		115.0
Length (overall): Station Wagons		199.9
Other Models		197.0
Width (overall)		75.0
Height (loaded): Sedans		53.0
Sport Coupes		51.9
Convertibles		52.8
Station Wagons		54.6
Tread: Front		58.0
Rear		58.0
Interior Room (4-Door Sedan*):	**Front**	**Rear**
Torso Room	38.5	37.3
Leg Room	41.9	36.0
Hip Room	59.9	59.9
Shoulder Room	58.8	58.7
Entrance Height	29.7	29.3
Luggage Compartment Volume (cu ft): Total		27.8
Usable		17.1
Station Wagon Cargo Volume (cu ft)		86.0
Tires:		
SS 396 models and Station Wagons		7.75 x 14
Malibu Sport Sedan (V8), Convertibles and models with 275-hp V8 engine		7.35 x 14
Other Models		6.95 x 14
Turning Diameter (feet): Curb-to-curb		40.3
Wall-to-wall		43.1
Steering Ratio (overall): Standard		28.0:1
Power Steering		20.4:1
Curb Weight (lbs)—Chevelle 300 4-Door Sedan*: 6-cyl		3085
V8		3235

*See Finger-Tip Facts for other models.

1966 specifications.

Interior Trim Codes:

B—Blue
D—Red
E—Black
F—Fawn
L—Optional Black Vinyl
R—Bright Blue
S—White/Black
T—Turquoise
V—Optional Fawn Vinyl
Z—Bronze

INTERIOR TRIM

SOLID EXTERIOR COLORS & CODE		SS 396: Super Sport Coupe, Super Sport Convertible (Vinyl)							SS 396 and Malibu with Strato-Bucket Seats: Sport Coupes and Convertibles (Vinyl)						Malibu: Sedans and Coupe (Cloth) / Wagons and Convertible (Vinyl)				Malibu			Chevelle 300 and 300 Deluxe: Chevelle 300 All Models (Cloth) / 300 Deluxe Sedans (Cloth), Station Wagon (Vinyl)			
		Fawn	White/Black	Red	Turquoise	Bronze	Black	Bright Blue	Fawn	Red	Bronze	Black	Bright Blue	White/Black	Fawn	Turquoise	Red	Blue	Black Vinyl—Convertible only	Bronze Vinyl—Convertible only	Opt. Black Vinyl—Spt. Cpe. & Sdn.	Fawn	Blue	Red	Opt. Fawn Vinyl—300 Sedans
Tuxedo Black	AA	F	S	D	T	Z	E	R	F	D	Z	E	R	S	F	T	D	B	E	Z	L	F	B	D	V
Ermine White	CC	F	S	D	T	Z	E	R	F	D	Z	E	R	S	F	T	D	B	E	Z	L	F	B	D	V
Mist Blue	DL	F•	S				E		F•			E		S	F			B	E		L		B		
Danube Blue	EE	F•					E		F•			E			F			B	E		L		B		
Marina Blue	FF		S				E	R				E	R	S				B•	E		L		B•		
Willow Green	HH	F•	S				E		F•			E		S	F				E		L	F			V
Artesian Turquoise	KK	F•	S		T		E		F•			E		S	F	T			E		L	F			V
Tropic Turquoise	LL	F•			T				F•						F	T						F			V
Aztec Bronze	MM	F				Z	E		F		Z	E			F				E	Z	L	F			V
Madeira Maroon	NN	F	S	D			E		F	D		E		S	F		D		E		L	F		D	V
Regal Red	RR		S	D			E			D		E		S			D		E		L			D	
Sandalwood Tan	TT	F					E		F			E			F				E		L	F			V
Cameo Beige	VV	F				Z	E		F		Z	E			F				E	Z	L	F			V
Chateau Slate	WW		S				E	R•				E	R•	S				B•	E		L		B•		
Lemonwood Yellow	YY	F•	S		T•		E		F•			E		S	F•	T•			E		L	F•			V•

• SPECIAL NOTE: Trim codes marked with a dot (•) are qualified "acceptable" rather than recommended. Both dealer and customer should consider this qualification before ordering.

TWO-TONE EXTERIOR COMBINATION & CODE
(Not available on Convertible models)

Ermine White/Artesian Turquoise	CK				T											T									
Mist Blue/Ermine White	DC																	B					B		
Mist Blue/Danube Blue	DE																	B					B		
Tropic Turquoise/Ermine White	LC				T											T									
Madeira Maroon/Tuxedo Black	NA						E					E							E		L				
Sandalwood Tan/Cameo Beige	TV	F							F						F							F			V
Chateau Slate/Tuxedo Black	WA						E					E							E		L				

Color and trim selections for 1966.

CHAPTER FOUR
Only Slight Revisions

The popular styling of the 1966 Chevelles continued into the 1967 models with only minor changes. However, one new model did appear, the Concours, which was just a dolled-up wagon featuring a wood-grain appliqué. With this prestige unit the Malibu wagon became the middle-of-the-line model. Chevelle's economy wagon still was the 300 DeLuxe, which continued to be available in six-passenger form. All other models remained in the line-up for the year.

Chevelle's standard SS 396 engine for 1967 again developed 325 hp but the optional 396 Turbo-Jet engine for the 396 SS cars developed 350 hp, ten fewer horsepower than the 1966 cars. These cars could do 0-60 in 6.5 seconds, and in 14.9 seconds be a quarter of a mile down the road. The compression ratio was 10.25:1; dual exhausts came as standard equipment. Premium fuel again was required for both versions of the 396 engine.

The two 396s had some differences, also: The 325 hp engine turned over at 4800 rpm, torque was 410 pounds-feet at 3200 rpm and a general-performance

Here is a 1967 300 DeLuxe four-door sedan showing the fancier exterior trim. It wears the deluxe wheel covers which sold for $17.40 per set of four. The part number was 986801. This unit tells us it's a V-8 by the V emblem on the front left-hand corner.

camshaft was used. The 350 hp engine turned over at 5200 rpm, the torque was 415 pounds-feet at 3400 rpm and a high-performance camshaft was required.

In addition to the engines listed above, Chevelle also offered limited editions (never cataloged) of a 396 engine that developed 375 hp at 5600 rpm. It had a compression ratio of 11.00:1 using the regular four-barrel carburetor.

The 350 hp 327 was down-rated to 325 hp this year, but was still offered. Few were ordered. The 275 hp 327, however, was often found in Chevelles.

Motion Performance used the SS 396 for conversion to the SS 427 that year which was fairly common for street performances.

Among new chassis items for 1967 was a power front disc brake option, which brought with it a set of four distinctive silver slotted rims, with trim rings and center caps. A new, more squared front and rear treatment was used. The 1967 Chevelle taillights wrapped around the fender caps, a safety feature reflecting the pressure of impending government mandates. Body dimensions of the cars were the same as 1966 models.

Tire sizes for the 1967 Chevelles were F-70x14 redlines for the SS 396 models and 7.75x14 standard on the sport sedan, Malibu convertible and wagons. All other models required 7.35x14 tires.

The factory-installed optional equipment for the 1967 Chevelles is listed in this chapter.

Chevelle production was not as terrific as it had been in 1966. The company produced 369,100 units, of which 24,700 were in the 300 series. Most of these—19,900—used six-cylinder powerplants; the remaining 4,800 came as V-8s. There were 26,300 in the 300 DeLuxe series. Again the six-cylinder models took precedence with 19,300 being built; the remaining 7,000 came off the assembly line as V-8s. In the Malibu series 187,200 used the V-8 and only 40,600 saw life as a six. The SS 396 used the V-8 which accounted for the 63,000 produced. Wagon production was 27,300 and, of this number, 21,400 came with the V-8 powerplant.

Prices ranged from $2,326 for model 13211 (better known as the Chevelle 300 two-door sedan) to $3,206 for the SS 396 convertible, model 13867.

The 1967 Malibu station wagon sports the accessory wheel discs and whitewall tires. It was referred to as Model 13635 and sold for $2,801. The body-to-frame mountings were cushioned in rubber to give a quieter ride.

This was the most expensive Chevelle sedan in 1967. It sold for $2,506 as a V-8 and weighed 3,130 pounds. It also was the most popular sedan in the Chevelle line.

Definitely the plushest interior in the entire 1967 Chevelle line went to the Malibu sport sedan, as shown here.

Seen here is the Malibu sport sedan in its second year of four-door hardtop styling. This model wears the accessory wheel covers, whitewall tires and vinyl roof. In base form it sold for $2,611 and weighed 3,200 pounds. The vinyl roof covering sold for $74.

A three-quarter rear view of the newest model for the year, the Concours six-passenger, two-seat wagon. The luggage rack carrier, part number 987053, had a suggested list price of $33.25. Note the special ribbed rocker molding (which came only on this and the SS 396) and the wood-grain appliqué.

A real mover was the SS 396 convertible. It weighed 3,435 pounds and sold new for $3,206. Red-line tires were part of the standard package on the SS 396 cars.

The popular SS 396 sport coupe weighed 3,435 pounds and retailed for $2,999. Note the SS emblem on the grille and the louvered hood to help distinguish it from the other models for the year.

In case you were wondering, I've always been "gone" on '67 Chevelles, especially the SS 396. This rear view, I guess, sums it all up pretty well. Its deeply recessed rear window line, the SS emblems placed below the trunk lid, red-line tires and the sculptured taillamp treatment make for one of the nicest-looking Chevelles ever built.

This is the factory stock deluxe wheel cover used on 1967 Chevelle models.

This completely stock 1967 Chevelle Malibu sport coupe carries a 283 ci engine under its hood. When equipped with the small V-8 it sold for $2,793.

The front fender designation for a 1967 Chevelle using the 283 ci V-8.

This interior view of a 1967 Chevelle shows some unusual options, such as the floor tachometer.

Malibu designations were mounted on the rear quarter panels for the 1967 models. The taillamps were more rounded than on the 1966 cars with wraparound fender cap giving more illumination at night.

The front end of a 1967 Chevelle was very similar to the 1966 model except that the grille bars were placed farther apart.

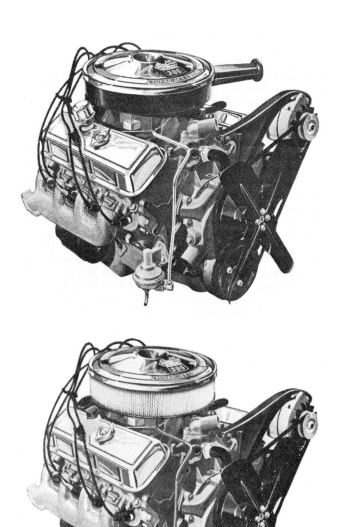

This clean 396 Turbo-Jet engine that develops 350 horsepower is from one of the cars in the collection of Len Cormier, of Cormier Chevrolet in Long Beach, California.

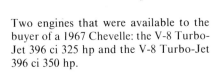

Two engines that were available to the buyer of a 1967 Chevelle: the V-8 Turbo-Jet 396 ci 325 hp and the V-8 Turbo-Jet 396 ci 350 hp.

In addition to the regular, large accessory wheel disc, Chevelle offered its customers mag-style wheel covers, simulated wire wheel covers and Rally wheel covers.

An interior view of a basic 1967 Chevelle Malibu with all-vinyl trim.

A view of the 396 Turbo-Jet flags used on cars so equipped for 1967.

A basic 283 V-8 engine that sees daily use is mounted into the engine compartment of this 1967 Chevelle.

Left column

	Part No.
AIR CONDITIONING, COMFORT-CAR	
230-cu.-in. 6-cylinder	987018
283-cu. in. and 327-cu.-in. V8	987019
396-cu.-in. V8 (with Automatic trans.)	987020
AIR CONDITIONING ADAPTER	
For 6-cylinder with Power Steering	985747
For use with 987019 and GM Air Injection Reactor	987097
For use with 987020 and GM Air Injection Reactor	987075
ANTENNA, MANUAL	
Right Front—AM-FM Radio	986463
Right Front—All Except AM-FM Radio	986902
Right Rear—Except AM-FM and Wagons	987039
BRAKES, POWER	986798
CAP, LOCKING GAS FILLER	
Station Wagon models	985895
Other models	985894
CARRIER, DECK LID	986914
CARRIER, LUGGAGE—Station Wagon	985806
CLOCK, ELECTRIC	986452
COMPASS	987092
COVER, LUGGAGE CARRIER	987053
DEFLECTOR, REAR WINDOW—Station Wagons	986430
DEFROSTER, REAR WINDOW	
All Sedan and Sport Coupe models	986942
EMERGENCY ROAD KIT	986792
EXTINGUISHER, FIRE—2¾-lb. dry chemical	985592
EXTINGUISHER, REFILL CARTRIDGE	985593
FAN, TEMPERATURE-CONTROLLED	
396-cu.-in. V8	986067
283- and 327-cu.-in. V8s	985355
FLOOR MAT, CLEAR VINYL—Full-width	
Front	986997
Rear	986998
FLOOR MAT, CONTOUR RUBBER—Front	
Turquoise 986987	Blue 986988
Black 986986	Red 986985
Gold 986989	Maroon 986990
FLOOR MAT, CONTOUR RUBBER—Rear	
Turquoise 986993	Blue 986994
Black 986992	Red 986991
Gold 986995	Maroon 986996
GUARDS, FRONT BUMPER	986836
GUARDS, REAR BUMPER—Except Wagons	986837
GUARDS, DOOR EDGE	
2-Door models	986647
4-Door models	986648
HORN, TRI-VOLUME	986966
LIGHTS	
Ashtray	986877
Glove Compartment—Standard on Concours, SS 396 and Malibu	986916
Luggage Compartment	986876
Underhood	987028
Courtesy—Standard on Convertible	986938
LITTER CONTAINER—Instrument Panel Mounted	986670
LITTER CONTAINER—Saddle Type	
Black 986607	Blue 986602
Fawn 986603	Red 986608
LOCK BUTTON, SAFETY—Rear Door	987103
LOCK, SPARE WHEEL	987048
MIRROR—Vanity Visor	987029
RACK, SKI—Requires Deck Lid Carrier	987066
RADIO EQUIPMENT	
Manual AM, Front Antenna	986849
Manual AM, Rear Antenna	986905
Pushbutton AM, Front Antenna	986850

Middle column

Pushbutton AM, Rear Antenna	986908
Pushbutton AM-FM, Front Antenna	986851
SPEAKER, REAR SEAT	
Station Wagons	986892
Other models	986891
SPEED CONTROL, CRUISE-MASTER	
For V8 with automatic transmissions	987032
SPEED CONTROL ADAPTER—For use with 987032 and 3- or 4-Speed transmission	987031
SPOTLIGHT, HAND PORTABLE	987112
SPOTLIGHT, REMOTE-CONTROL	986940
SPOTLIGHT ADAPTER—For right-hand installation of Remote-Control Unit	986941
STEREO, MULTIPLEX SYSTEM	
Multiplex	986975
Front speaker	987059
Rear speakers (2)—Wagons	986892
Others	986891
Speaker housings—Convertible (2)	987056
Station Wagons (RH)	987058
STEREO, SWITCH—For use when both Multiplex and Tape System installed	987077
STEREO TAPE PLAYER	
Tape player	987063
Front speaker	987059

Right column

Rear speakers (2)—Wagons	986892
Others	986891
Speaker housings—Convertible (2)	987056
Station Wagons (RH)	987058
TACHOMETER	987099
TISSUE DISPENSER—Instrument panel mounted	986965
TRAILER HITCH	
Station Wagons	986455
Other models	986420
TRAILER WIRING HARNESS	
Station Wagons	987047
Other models	987046
VENTSHADES	
4-Door Sedans	986778
Station Wagons	986795
WHEEL COVERS—Set of four—14". Not available with Front Disc Brakes	
SS 396	986801
Other models	986807
WHEEL COVERS, MAG-STYLE—Not available with Front Disc Brakes	
Set of four—14"	987067
WHEEL COVERS, SIMULATED WIRE—Not available with Front Disc Brakes	
Set of four—14"	987100

Dealer-installed custom feature accessories for 1967.

Chevelle specifications for 1967.

	SS 396		CONCOURS	MALIBU						CHEVELLE 300 DELUXE			CHEVELLE 300	
CARGO COMPARTMENT	Sport Coupe	Conv.	Custom Wagon	Sport Sedan	Sport Coupe	Conv.	4-Dr. Sedan	2-Seat Wagon	4-Dr. Sedan	2-Dr. Sedan	2-Seat Wagon	4-Dr. Sedan	2-Dr. Sedan
Floor Length—Front Seat to Tailgate	—		92.1*	—				92.1*	—		92.1*	—	
Floor Length—2nd Seat to Tailgate	—		59.1	—				59.1	—		59.1	—	
Maximum Load Floor Width	—		59.6	—				59.6	—		59.6	—	
Width between Wheelhouses	—		42.4	—				42.4	—		42.4	—	
Height—Floor to Roof (max.)	—		31.3	—				31.3	—		31.3	—	
Tailgate Loading Height	—		26.9	—				26.9	—		26.9	—	
Tailgate Opening Height	—		28.5	—				28.5	—		28.5	—	
Tailgate Opening Width at Floor	—		54.6	—				54.6	—		54.6	—	
Tailgate Opening Width at Belt	—		52.5	—				52.5	—		52.5	—	
Total Cargo Volume (cu. ft.)	—		86.0	—				86.0	—		86.0	—	
GLASS AREA													
Windshield Glass Area (sq. in.)	1144.2		1107.1	1107.1	1144.2		1107.1		1107.1			1107.1	
Rear Window Glass Area (sq. in.)	728.9	833.8	768.4	812.8	728.9	833.8	935.1	768.4	935.1		768.4	935.1	
Total Glass Area (sq. in.)	3145.3	3186.6	4374.1	3352.7	3145.3	3816.6	3320.2	4374.1	3320.2	3395.8	4374.1	3320.2	3395.8
TIRE SIZE & STEERING SPECIFICATIONS (For additional information, see Tires in Feature Details section.)													
Standard Tire Size—6 cyl.	—		(b)	(b)	(a)	(b)	(a)	(b)	(a)		(b)	(a)	
—V8	(c)		(b)	(b)	(a)	(b)	(a)	(b)	(a)		(b)	(a)	
Turning Circle—Curb-to-Curb (ft.)	40.3		40.3	40.3					40.3			40.3	
Turning Circle—Wall-to-Wall (ft.)	43.1		43.1	43.1					43.1			43.1	
Steering Ratio—Std. (overall)	28.0:1		28.0:1	28.0:1					28.0:1			28.0:1	
Steering Ratio—Power (overall)	20.4:1		20.4:1	20.4:1					20.4:1			20.4:1	
FUEL CAPACITY & WEIGHT													
Fuel Tank Capacity (gallons)	20		20	20					20			20	
Curb Weight—Six (lbs.)	—	—	3430	3200	3115	3200	3135	3420	3115	3090	3385	3095	3075
Curb Weight—V8 (lbs.)	3585	3655	3560	3345	3250	3330	3270	3550	3250	3225	3520	3230	3210
Shipping Weight—Six (lbs.)	—	—	3270	3055	2970	3050	2990	3260	2970	2945	3230	2945	2925
Shipping Weight—V8 (lbs.)	3415	3495	3405	3200	3100	3185	3120	3390	3100	3080	3360	3080	3060

*Tailgate open—114.5   (a) 7.35 x 14   (b) 7.75 x 14   (c) F70 x 14

Chevelle Factory-Installed Optional* Equipment
for all Chevelle models except as otherwise specified

POWER TEAMS

RPO

ENGINES—All models except SS 396:

155-hp Turbo-Thrift 250 6-cyl. L22

275-hp Turbo-Fire 327 V8—Includes heavier springs, heavier duty clutch, 61-ampere-hour battery and higher performance starting motor L30

325-hp Turbo-Fire 327 V8—Includes heavier springs, dual exhausts, heavier duty clutch, 61-ampere-hour battery, higher performance starting motor, and special chrome accents L79

SS 396 models only:

350-hp Turbo-Jet 396 V8—Includes heavier springs and shock absorbers, heavier front stabilizer, rear suspension frame reinforcement, 8.875" diameter ring gear, dual exhausts, 61-ampere-hour battery, high flow air cleaner, higher performance starting motor, and special chrome accents L34

TRANSMISSIONS

Powerglide—Available on all except RPO L79 325-hp engine M35

Turbo Hydra-Matic — Available with both Turbo-Jet 396 V8 engines M40

4-Speed Fully Synchronized — (Wide Range). Available with all V8 engines M20

4-Speed Fully Synchronized—(Close ratio). Available with 325-hp (RPO L79) and 350-hp engines . M21

Special 3-Speed Fully Synchronized — Standard with all SS 396 engines and available with all other six and V8 engines M13

Overdrive — Available with both 6-cylinder engines and 195-hp V8 . . . . M10

AXLE, POSITRACTION REAR—Available with all axle ratios G80

AXLE RATIOS — For availability of Economy, Performance, or Special axle ratios consult Power Teams chart.

POWER ASSISTS

BRAKES, POWER J50

SEATS, POWER 4-WAY—For conventional front seats. Not available on Chevelle 300 or models with bucket seats or floor-mounted transmission . . A41

STEERING, POWER N40

WINDOWS, POWER—All but Chevelle 300 and 300 Deluxe models A31

FEATURE GROUPS

(All items in Groups may be ordered separately.)

APPEARANCE GUARD GROUP—Includes three or more of the following items: 1. Front and Rear Floor Mats 2. Front Bumper Guards 3. Custom Deluxe Seat Belts 4. Door Edge Guards 5. Rear Bumper Guards.
Concours Custom Wagon . . . . (1, 2, 3)
300 Deluxe and Malibu Wagons . . . . . . (1, 2, 3, 4)
Sedans, Coupes and Convertibles . . . (1, 2, 3, 4, 5)

AUXILIARY LIGHTING GROUP—Includes three or more of the following items: 1. Courtesy Lights 2. Underhood Light 3. Ashtray Light 4. Luggage Compartment Light 5. Glove Compartment Light.
Convertibles . . . . (2, 3, 4)
Concours and Malibu Wagons . . . . (1, 2, 3)
Malibu Sedans and all Sport Coupes . (1, 2, 3, 4)
300 Deluxe Wagons . . . . (1, 2, 3, 5)
300 and 300 Deluxe Sedans . . . . (1, 2, 3, 4, 5)

FOUNDATION GROUP—Includes Pushbutton Radio, Electric Clock and Extra-Thick Foam Front Seat Cushion. 300 and 300 Deluxe models only.

OPERATING CONVENIENCE GROUP—Includes Outside Remote Control Rearview Mirror and Rear Window Defroster for all except Wagons.

STATION WAGON CONVENIENCE GROUP—Includes Luggage Carrier, Power Rear Window, and Rear Window Air Deflector. All Wagon models.

EXTERIOR FEATURES

GUARDS, DOOR EDGE—Except Custom Wagons . . B93

GUARDS, FRONT BUMPER—All models V31

GUARDS, REAR BUMPER—Except Wagons V32

MIRROR, OUTSIDE REMOTE CONTROL D33

MOLDINGS, SIDE WINDOW — 4-Door Sedans plus Malibu and 300 Deluxe Station Wagons B90

RPO

ROOF COVER, VINYL—Hardtop models only. Black or beige vinyl with any exterior color. . . . C08

STRIPES, SPECIAL BODY ACCENT — Replace the standard stripes on SS 396 models D96

TIRES:
Note: Base tire sizes are as follows:

Std. 6 and V8	275-hp V8	325-hp V8
SS 396—F70 x 14	Same as std. ex-	SS 396—F70 x 14
Wagons—7.75 x 14	cept Malibu Sport	Others—7.75 x 14
Others—7.35 x 14	Sedan & Conver-	
	tible—7.75 x 14	

For additional information, see Tires in Feature Details section.

7.25 x 14—Whitewall, original equipment 2-ply tubeless. All except Wagons and SS 396 models . P58

7.75 x 14—Blackwall, original equipment 2-ply tubeless. Standard on Wagons, available for all other models except SS 396 . . . . P65

7.75 x 14—Whitewall, original equipment 2-ply tubeless. All except SS 396 . . . . P62

7.75 x 14—Blackwall, original equipment 4-ply tubeless. Wagons only T14

7.75 x 14—Whitewall, original equipment 4-ply tubeless. Wagons only T15

F70 x 14—Red Stripe, special nylon 2-ply tubeless. All except SS 396 and Wagons PW8

F70 x 14—White Stripe, special nylon 2-ply tubeless. All except Wagons PW7

TOP, CONVERTIBLE—Choice of white, black, or blue. See Sales Album, Colors and Fabrics section C05

TOP, POWER-OPERATED CONVERTIBLE C05/C06

TWO-TONE FINISH—See Sales Album, Colors and Fabrics section, for samples and availability.

WHEEL COVERS — Set of four. Not available with Front Disc Brakes P01

WHEEL COVERS, MAG-STYLE—Set of four. Not available with Front Disc Brakes N96

WHEEL COVERS, SIMULATED WIRE—Set of four. Not available with Front Disc Brakes P02

INTERIOR FEATURES

AIR CONDITIONING, FOUR-SEASON—Heater and air conditioner combined. Includes Heavy-Duty Radiator, Temperature-Controlled Fan, and 61-ampere-hour Delcotron Generator. 7.75 x 14 or larger tires must be ordered where they are not standard equipment C60

BELTS, SEAT—In addition to or replacing standard seat belts. Center Rear—For use with standard seat belts. Sedans and Wagons A68
Custom Deluxe—Front (2) and rear (2) A39
Custom Deluxe Center Rear—Requires RPO A39. Sedans and Wagons AL5

BELTS, FRONT SHOULDER
For use with standard seat belts. AS1
Custom Deluxe—Requires RPO A39 . . . . A85

CLOCK, ELECTRIC—300 and 300 Deluxe models. . U35

CONSOLE – Available only when Strato-bucket seats are ordered. Includes electric clock, rear seat courtesy light, and stowage compartment. Not available with Overdrive or standard 3-Speed (except with SS 396 models) D55

DEFROSTER, REAR WINDOW—Available only on Sedans and Sport Coupes. Not available with Stereo Tape System C50

GLASS, SOFT-RAY TINTED—All windows A01
Windshield only A02

HEADRESTS, STRATO-EASE—Front seat only
With Strato-bucket seats A81
With standard seats A82

INSTRUMENTATION, SPECIAL—Available on V8 Sport Coupe and Convertible models. Includes tachometer plus ammeter, temperature and oil pressure gauges U14

LIGHTS
Ashtray U28
Courtesy—All except Convertible models U29
Glove Compartment—300 and 300 Deluxe models . U27
Luggage Compartment U25
Underhood U26

MATS, FLOOR—Color-keyed front (2) and rear (2) B37

RPO

RADIO EQUIPMENT
Radios, Pushbutton—With front antenna:
AM Radio U63
AM Radio and Rear Seat Speaker U63/U80
AM-FM Radio U69
AM-FM Radio and Rear Seat Speaker U69/U80
Antenna, Rear—Not available with AM-FM Radio or Wagon models. Manual U73
Speaker, Rear Seat—For use with Foundation Group only U80

SEAT CUSHION, EXTRA-THICK FOAM—Front seat for 300 and 300 Deluxe models B55

SEATS, STRATO - BUCKET – Available on Sport Coupe and Convertible models A51

SPEED CONTROL, CRUISE-MASTER—Available with V8 models when Powerglide is ordered K30

SPEED WARNING INDICATOR U15

STEERING WHEEL, COMFORTILT – Available on models equipped with automatic or 4-Speed transmission N33

STEERING WHEEL, DELUXE—300 and 300 Deluxe . N30

STEERING WHEEL, SPORTS-STYLED N34

STEREO TAPE SYSTEM – Includes four speakers. Not available when radio with rear seat speaker is ordered U57

TRIM, INTERIOR—See Color and Trim Section for colors and codes.
Deluxe all-vinyl—Malibu Sport Coupe and Sport Sedan
Deluxe cloth—Malibu Sport Sedan
All-vinyl (Fawn and Black)—Chevelle 300

Extra Cost

WAGON FEATURES

RPO

AIR DEFLECTOR, REAR WINDOW C51

CARRIER, LUGGAGE V55

WINDOW, POWER TAILGATE A33

HEAVY-DUTY AND OTHER EQUIPMENT

BATTERY, HEAVY-DUTY—70-ampere-hour rating . T60

BRAKES, FRONT DISC — Includes special hub cap and trim ring. Not available with Sintered Metallic Brake Linings J52

BRAKE LININGS, SINTERED METALLIC J65

CLUTCH, HEAVY-DUTY—Not available on SS 396 models, with 155-hp 6-cylinder engine, or GM Air Injection Reactor M01

ENGINE VENTILATION, CLOSED POSITIVE-TYPE Not available with 325-hp (L79) or 350-hp V8's . . K24

EXHAUST, DUAL—275-hp V8 engine N10

FAN, TEMPERATURE-CONTROLLED—For V8 engine models only. Included with Air Conditioning . . K02

GENERATOR, DELCOTRON:
12-42-Ampere—Not available with Air Conditioning K79
5-61-Ampere—Included with Air Conditioning . K76

GM AIR INJECTION REACTOR—Requires Closed Engine Positive Ventilation. For California registered vehicles only K19

HEATER AND DEFROSTER DELETION—Credit option. Not available with Air Conditioning C48

HORN, TRI-VOLUME—Except Chevelle 300 models U03

RADIATOR, HEAVY-DUTY—Included with Air Conditioning V01

SHOCK ABSORBERS, SUPERLIFT AIR-ADJUSTABLE Rear only G66

SUSPENSION, SPECIAL FRONT AND REAR—Wagon models: special front and rear springs. Other models: special front and rear springs and shock absorbers F40

TACHOMETER—V8 models only U16

1967 factory-installed optional equipment.

Left Interior Color Table

Interior Trim Codes:
- E – Black
- B – Blue
- G – Gold
- D – Red
- T – Turquoise
- M – Maroon
- R – Bright Blue
- L – *Opt. Black Vinyl
- U – *Opt. Blue Vinyl
- A – *Opt. Red Vinyl
- H – *Opt. Bright Blue Vinyl

INTERIOR COLOR AND CODE

EXTERIOR COLOR	CODE	CONCOURS CUSTOM WAGON ALL-VINYL					SS 396 SPORT COUPE CONVERTIBLE (standard and *optional Strato-bucket seats) ALL-VINYL						MALIBU SPORT COUPE SPORT SEDAN 4-DOOR SEDAN (standard seat) CLOTH					MALIBU SPORT COUPE SPORT SEDAN (*optional all-vinyl trim) ALL-VINYL			
		Black	Blue	Red	Gold	Turquoise	Black	Blue	Red	Gold	Turquoise	Bright Blue	Black	Blue	Turquoise	Gold	Maroon	Black	Blue (Sedan only)	Red (Coupe only)	Bright Blue (Coupe only)
Tuxedo Black	AA	E	B	D	G	T	E	B	D	G	T	R	E	B	T	G	M	L	U	A	H
Ermine White	CC	E	B	D	G	T	E	B	D	G	T	R	E	B	T	G	M	L	U	A	H
Nantucket Blue	DD	E	B				E	B					E	B				L	U		
Deepwater Blue	EE	E	B				E	B					E	B				L	U		
Marina Blue	FF	B					E	B				R	E	B				L	U		H
Granada Gold	GG	E			G		E			G			E			G		L			
Mountain Green	HH	E					E						E					L			
Emerald Turquoise	KK	E				T	E				T		E		T			L			
Tahoe Turquoise	LL	E				T	E				T		E		T			L			
Royal Plum	MM	E					E						E					L			
Madeira Maroon	NN	E		D	G		E		D	G			E			G	M	L		A	
Bolero Red	RR	E		D			E		D				E					L		A	
Sierra Fawn	SS	E			G		E			G			E			G		L			
Capri Cream	TT	E			G		E			G			E			G		L			
Butternut Yellow	YY	E				T	E				T		E		T			L			

TWO-TONE EXTERIOR COMBINATIONS* & CODE (Not available on Convertibles)

		CONCOURS	SS 396	MALIBU CLOTH	MALIBU VINYL
Ermine White/Nantucket Blue	CD	Two-tone combinations not available	B	B	U
Nantucket Blue/Ermine White	DC		B	B	U
Deepwater Blue/Nantucket Blue	ED		B	B	U
Nantucket Blue/Deepwater Blue	DE		B	B	U
Granada Gold/Capri Cream	GT		E G	E G	L
Tahoe Turquoise/Ermine White	LC		T	T	
Sierra Fawn/Capri Cream	ST		E G	E G	L

*Optional at extra cost.   29

SPECIAL NOTE: Trim codes shown are recommended; however, any solid exterior color may be ordered with any interior.

Right Interior Color Table

Interior Trim Codes:
- E – Black
- B – Blue
- G – Gold
- D – Red
- T – Turquoise
- R – Bright Blue
- F – Fawn
- N – *Opt. Black Cloth
- S – *Opt. Blue Cloth
- W – *Opt. Gold Cloth
- P – *Opt. Plum Cloth
- V – *Opt. Fawn Vinyl

INTERIOR COLOR AND CODE

CODE	EXTERIOR COLOR	MALIBU SPORT SEDAN (*optional Deluxe interior) CLOTH				MALIBU SPORT SEDAN CONVERTIBLE (*optional Strato-bucket seats) ALL-VINYL				MALIBU CONVERTIBLE STATION WAGON (standard seat) ALL-VINYL						300 DELUXE SEDANS CLOTH			300 DELUXE STATION WAGON ALL-VINYL		300 SEDANS CLOTH	300 *Opt. VINYL
		Black	Blue	Gold	Plum	Black	Blue	Red	Bright Blue	Black	Blue	Red	Gold	Turquoise	Bright Blue (Conv. only)	Black	Blue	Fawn	Blue	Fawn	Black	Fawn
AA	Tuxedo Black	N	S	W	P	E	B	D	R	E	B	D	G	T	R	E	B	F	B	F	E	V
CC	Ermine White	N	S	W	P	E	B	D	R	E	B	D	G	T	R	E	B	F	B	F	E	V
DD	Nantucket Blue	N	S			E	B			E	B					E	B		B		E	
EE	Deepwater Blue	N	S			E	B			E	B					E	B		B		E	
FF	Marina Blue	N	S			E	B			R	E	B				E	B		B		E	
GG	Granada Gold	N		W		E			G	E			G			E		F		F	E	V
HH	Mountain Green	N				E				E						E		F		F	E	V
KK	Emerald Turquoise	N				E			T	E				T		E		F		F	E	V
LL	Tahoe Turquoise	N				E			T	E				T		E		F		F	E	V
MM	Royal Plum	N			P	E				E						E				F	E	V
NN	Madeira Maroon	N				E		D	G	E		D	G			E		F		F	E	V
RR	Bolero Red	N				E		D		E		D				E				F	E	V
SS	Sierra Fawn	N		W		E			G	E			G			E		F		F	E	V
TT	Capri Cream	N		W		E			G	E			G			E		F		F	E	V
YY	Butternut Yellow	N				E				E				T		E		F		F	E	V

TWO-TONE EXTERIOR COMBINATIONS* & CODE

	CODE	EXTERIOR COLOR																				
CD	Ermine White/Nantucket Blue			S			B				B						B		B			
DC	Nantucket Blue/Ermine White			S			B				B						B		B			
ED	Deepwater Blue/Nantucket Blue			S			B				B						B					
DE	Nantucket Blue/Deepwater Blue			S			B				B						B					
GT	Granada Gold/Capri Cream	N		W		E			G	E			G			E		F		F	E	V
LC	Tahoe Turquoise/Ermine White								T													
ST	Sierra Fawn/Capri Cream	N		W		E			G	E			G			E		F		F	E	V

Black or Beige vinyl roof cover (RPO C08) available on all Sport Coupe and Sport Sedan models. *Optional at extra cost. Convertible folding top available in a choice of Black, White, or Blue.

1967 exterior color and interior trim choices.

Available Power Teams

ENGINE	TRANSMISSION	REAR AXLE RATIO MODEL APPLICATION	REAR AXLE RATIO Without Air Conditioning				With Air Conditioning			
			Standard	Economy†	Perform-ance†	Special†	Standard	Economy†	Perform-ance†	Special†
STANDARD 6 140-HP TURBO-THRIFT 230 230-CU.-IN. SIX NOT AVAILABLE ON SS 396	3-Speed (2.85:1 Low) Special 3-Speed (2.86:1 Low)	All models	3.36:1	3.08:1	3.55:1	3.70:1	3.36:1		3.55:1	3.70:1
	Overdrive	All models	3.70:1				3.70:1			
	Powerglide	All models except Wagons	3.08:1*		3.36:1	3.55:1 3.70:1	3.36:1		3.55:1	3.70:1
		Wagons	3.36:1	3.08:1	3.55:1	3.70:1	3.36:1		3.55:1	3.70:1
RPO L22 155-HP TURBO-THRIFT 250 250-CU.-IN. SIX NOT AVAILABLE ON SS 396	3-Speed (2.85:1 Low) Special 3-Speed (2.86:1 Low)	All models	3.08:1		3.36:1	3.55:1 3.70:1	3.36:1		3.55:1	3.70:1
	Overdrive	All models	3.70:1				3.70:1			
	Powerglide	All models except Wagons	3.08:1		3.36:1	3.55:1 3.70:1	3.36:1		3.55:1	3.70:1
		Wagons	3.36:1	3.08:1	3.55:1	3.70:1	3.36:1		3.55:1	3.70:1
STANDARD V8 195-HP TURBO-FIRE 283 283-CU.-IN. V8 NOT AVAILABLE ON SS 396	3-Speed (2.85:1 Low) Special 3-Speed (2.86:1 Low) 4-Speed (3.11:1 Low)	All models	3.08:1		3.36:1	3.55:1 3.70:1	3.36:1		3.55:1	3.70:1
	Overdrive	All models	3.70:1				3.70:1			
	Powerglide	All models	3.08:1		3.36:1	3.55:1 3.70:1	3.36:1		3.55:1	3.70:1
RPO L30 275-HP TURBO-FIRE 327 327-CU.-IN. V8 NOT AVAILABLE ON SS 396	3-Speed (2.54:1 Low) Special 3-Speed (2.41:1 Low) 4-Speed (2.54:1 Low)	All models	3.08:1		3.36:1	3.55:1 3.70:1	3.36:1		3.55:1	3.70:1
RPO L79 325-HP TURBO-FIRE 327 327-CU.-IN. V8 NOT AVAILABLE ON SS 396	Special 3-Speed (2.41:1 Low) 4-Speed (2.52:1 Low)	All models	3.31:1	3.07:1	3.55:1	3.73:1	3.31:1		3.55:1	3.73:1
	4-Speed (2.20:1 Low)	All models	3.31:1	3.07:1	3.55:1	**	3.31:1		3.55:1	3.73:1
SS 396 STANDARD V8 325-HP TURBO-JET 396 396-CU.-IN. V8 NOT AVAILABLE FOR CONCOURS, MALIBU, 300 DELUXE OR 300 SERIES MODELS	Special 3-Speed (2.41:1 Low) 4-Speed (2.52:1 Low)	All models	3.31:1	3.07:1	3.55:1	3.73:1 4.10:1	3.07:1			
	Powerglide	All models	3.07:1	2.73:1	3.31:1	3.55:1 3.73:1 4.10:1	3.07:1			
	◆Turbo Hydra-Matic	All models	2.73:1		3.07:1	3.31:1	3.07:1			
RPO L34 350-HP TURBO-JET 396 396-CU.-IN. V8 SS 396 ONLY	Special 3-Speed (2.41:1 Low) 4-Speed (2.52:1 Low)	All models	3.55:1	3.31:1	3.73:1	4.10:1	3.07:1			
	4-Speed (2.20:1 Low)	All models	3.55:1	3.31:1	3.73:1	**	3.07:1			
	Powerglide	All models	3.31:1	3.07:1	3.73:1	3.55:1 4.10:1	3.07:1			
	◆Turbo Hydra-Matic	All models	3.07:1	2.73:1	3.31:1		3.07:1			

Note: Positraction rear axle available in all axle ratios—required with 4.10:1, 4.56:1 and 4.88:1 ratios. †Optional—see Options & Accessories section.
**Choice of 3.07:1, 4.10:1, 4.56:1 or 4.88:1 ratios. ◆ Check availability before ordering.
*2.73:1 with G.M. Air Injection Reactor (RPO K19) unless 3.08:1 or other available ratios specified.

Available power teams this year.

CHAPTER FIVE
A Brand-New Body

In 1968, Chevrolet came out with a brand-new body style that would remain with the Chevelle models for the next five years. The Concours that was introduced in 1967 as a dolled-up station wagon now became available as a sport sedan. This was just a special trim package offered only on that model for $135 extra.

The sedan models resembled the hardtop sedans but did have more of a curve to the rear window than was seen in the hardtop version. All sedans increased in wheelbase length, to 116 inches, while other models used a new 112-inch wheelbase. The sedans had an overall length of 201 inches and the remaining models were 117 inches.

The number of models increased to fifteen but some were actually just trim versions of an existing model within the series. A low-production example with no special frills was the Nomad wagon. Gone from the line-up was the Chevelle 300 four-door sedan.

Standard Chevelles were again equipped with the faithful 230 ci six-cylinder or a new, 307 ci version of Chevrolet's beloved small-block. The SS 396 used the

A customer had the choice when ordering the SS 396 cars of receiving either the bench seat or the Strato-bucket seats.

same block as in the previous year: 396 ci developing 325 hp at 5200 rpm.

An engine option that appeared for the second year in a row, but was never cataloged in Chevrolet literature for 1968, was the 396 engine that developed 375 hp. It was placed in about 2,000 SS models. Used with the 396 engine was the M 13 Special three-speed, unless the extra-cost four-speed was ordered. Either the 2.41:1 low RPO M 20 or, for 350 and 375 hp cars, the 2.20:1 low M 21 box was found in many SS 396 cars. For those preferring an automatic, the faithful Powerglide was still available. However, many people were turning to the Turbo Hydra-matic as the tried-and-true transmission from GM. This three-speed automatic first appeared in Chevelles during 1967.

Regular equipment for the SS cars included finned front brake drums and bonded linings front and rear. Many of these models were equipped with the disc brake option which then included special slotted disc wheels with bright trim rings and center caps. The center cap was revised for 1968 to a style that would remain for several years. As a sidelight, the Chevrolet

assembly plant in Baltimore, Maryland, chose a 1968 SS 396 coupe as its car to commemorate the five-millionth Chevy assembled since the factory opened in 1935.

The SS 396 offered some quick identification marks to distinguish it from regular Malibu coupes and convertibles. The wheel covers carried the SS emblem in the center (unless the disc brake rims were used). A blacked-out grille had the SS emblems in the center. Many cars carried the optional stripes at the lower portion of the side panels directly above the rocker panel trim.

All SS and Malibu models came with the Hide-A-Way windshield wipers while the less-expensive Chevelles carried these only as optional equipment. Side-marker lights made their debut. In the fender nameplate with the marker light were the identifying numbers to indicate the engine displacement.

Tire size was 7.35x14 except on the wagons, convertibles and sport sedans which used 7.75x14 tires. SS 396 models came with F70x14 tires with red-line sidewalls.

The fuel tank capacity was twenty gallons.

The most expensive model among the 1968 Chevelles was the Concours estate wagon, which sold for $3,545 in three-seat, nine-passenger form.

A 1968 Malibu sport sedan sold for $3,085 and weighed 3,315 pounds. This version, displaying its Concours nameplate on the left front fender, was the newest sport sedan offered. It had a special trim package that cost an additional $135.

Chevelle prices ranged from $2,477 for the 300 coupe, model 13277, to $3,545 for a Concours nine-passenger estate wagon known as Model 13853.

The 1968 Chevelle 300 came with a choice of blue, gold or black vinyl interiors. The Chevelle 300 DeLuxe came with a fabric-vinyl combination in the same three colors. If one chose all-vinyl in a 300 DeLuxe, it was available in these same shades but of a richer-grain vinyl. Convertible tops were available in white, black or blue. Vinyl tops for sport coupes and sport sedans came in either black or white.

The 1968 Chevelle production figures increased over those of 1967. A total of 430,685 units was built. The 300 series sold 12,600, 2,900 of which were V-8s. The 300 DeLuxe line saw 43,200 produced with 25,500 coming off the line as six-cylinders and the remaining 17,700 using the V-8 powerplant. The Malibu line had a production of 266,300, including 233,200 V-8s and 33,100 six-cylinders. The SS 396 saw a production run of 62,785; of these 60,499 were coupes and 2,286 were convertibles. The remaining 45,500 were wagons; 34,800 came as V-8s and 10,700 used the six-cylinder powerplant.

This is my 1968 Malibu sport coupe when nearly new. It was purchased new by my sister in November of 1967 for $3,322.95. Today is has 115,000 miles, still looks good and still runs great—like a Chevy should.

The Malibu convertible was distinguished by its pinstripe along the center bodyline of the car. The rocker panel stainless trim did not continue on the rear quarter panel as on the SS 396. It was $239 less than the SS 396, selling for $3,214.

Here is a 1968 Chevelle Malibu four-door sedan that weighed 3,255 pounds and sold for $2,979 as a V-8.

A Malibu six-passenger wagon that sold for $3,302 and weighed 3,575 pounds. It also came in a nine-passenger version for $3,413. The roof rack was optional for $30.72, part number 987384.

Special Concours touches included the trunk emblem along with a fancier rear trim panel.

This is a deluxe wheel cover used on the regular 1966 Chevelle and Malibu models as an option. It sold for $17.25 per set of four. The wheel cutout trim was standard for the Malibu and Malibu Super Sport models.

Chevelle's lowest-priced hardtop came as this 300 DeLuxe sport coupe that weighed 3,185 pounds and sold for $2,584 with a six-cylinder engine. Note the distinguishing lack of a side-panel pinstripe and rear deck stainless trim; the rocker molding trim was at the base of the car rather than on the lower body panels as was the case for Malibu and SS 396. (The 300 DeLuxe Coupe looked similar with the addition of a center post.)

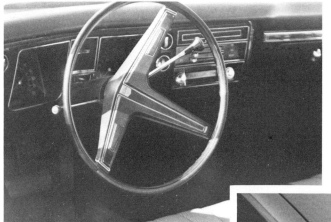

STANDARD ENGINES	3-SPEED FULLY SYNCH.	SPECIAL 3-SPEED FULLY SYNCH.	OVER-DRIVE	4-SPEED FULLY SYNCH.	POWER-GLIDE	TURBO HYDRA-MATIC
140-hp Turbo-Thrift 230**	x	x	x		x	
200-hp Turbo-Fire 307 V8**	x	x	x	x	x	
325-hp Turbo-Jet 396 V8*		x		x	x	x
EXTRA-COST ENGINES						
155-hp Turbo-Thrift 250	x	x	x		x	
250-hp Turbo-Fire 327 V8	x	x	x	x	x	
275-hp Turbo-Fire 327 V8	x	x		x	x	
325-hp Turbo-Fire 327 V8		x			x	
350-hp Turbo-Jet 396 V8*		x		x	x	x

**Standard engines for all but SS 396 models.   *Available only on SS 396 models.

1968 engine specifications.

The interior seat material was of excellent quality for the 1968 Chevelle Malibu. My car has over 115,000 miles and still has the original seat material. All dash instruments are easily seen by the driver. The steering wheel on SS 396 models looked almost identical to the Malibu's except for the SS emblem in the center.

This rear view of a 1968 Chevelle Malibu shows the accessory bumper-guard equipment. The accessory was part number 987197 and sold for $8.35 per pair. The back-up lamps were mounted within the bumper next to the guards.

TISSUE DISPENSER

CUSTOM MAGNESIUM WHEEL COVERS

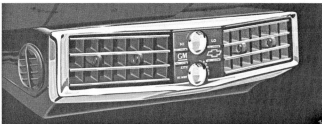

GM CHEVROLET AIR CONDITIONER

VINYL CONTOUR FLOOR MATS

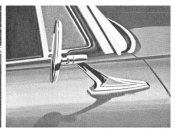

RIGHT HAND REAR VIEW MIRROR

TACHOMETER

SPARE WHEEL LOCK

CRUISE-MASTER SPEED CONTROL

DOOR EDGE GUARDS

TRAILER HITCH

LOCKING GASOLINE TANK CAP

FRONT & REAR BUMPER GUARDS

Various 1968 Chevelle accessories could be ordered to make a car more personalized.

The fender marker on this 1968 Chevelle denotes the 307 ci V-8. Side marker lights became standard this year. The wheel covers cost the buyer $17.40 per set of four. They carried a part number of 987250.

Pinstriping was part of the regular package on 1968 Chevelles. Windwings certainly appealed to me over the General Motors Astro Ventilation, which became common on most GM cars within the next two years. The outside rearview mirror was also standard equipment.

The front end of the 1968 Chevelle. Each of the quad lights carried its separate housing. The front bumper-guard equipment sold for $8.35 per pair and had a part number of 987203. The grille plaques are a "Moloney frill!"

A basic 307 engine block, which my 1968 Chevelle carries.

A view of the vinyl door paneling on a 1968 Malibu Sport coupe. All window and door cranks were easily accessible.

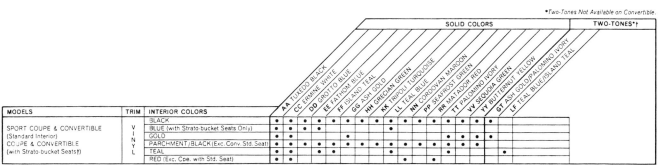

*Two-Tones Not Available on Wagon.

MODELS	TRIM	INTERIOR COLORS	AA TUXEDO BLACK	CC ERMINE WHITE	DD GROTTO BLUE	EE FATHOM BLUE	FF ISLAND TEAL	GG ASH GOLD	HH GRECIAN GREEN	KK TRIPOLI TURQUOISE	LL TEAL BLUE	NN CORDOVAN MAROON	PP SEAFROST GREEN	RR MATADOR RED	TT PALOMINO IVORY	VV SEQUOIA GREEN	YY BUTTERNUT YELLOW	DC GROTTO BLUE/ERMINE WHITE	DE GROTTO BLUE/FATHOM BLUE	ED FATHOM BLUE/GROTTO BLUE	GT ASH GOLD/PALOMINO IVORY
CONCOURS SPORT SEDAN (RPO ZJ6†) (Optional Interior for Malibu)	C L O T H	BLACK	•	•	•	•	•	•	•	•	•	•	•	•	•	•	•				
		BLUE	•	•						•								•	•	•	
		GOLD	•	•				•						•	•	•					•
		GRAY-GREEN	•	•		•			•		•				•						
ESTATE WAGON (Standard Interior)	V I N Y L	BLACK	•	•	•	•		•		•		•	•	•	•	•	•				
		BLUE	•	•	•	•				•											
		SADDLE	•	•			•				•	•		•							
		TURQUOISE	•	•					•												

†Optional at Extra Cost.

Concours estate wagon and Concours sport sedan colors and trim, 1968.

*Two-Tones Not Available on Convertible.

MODELS	TRIM	INTERIOR COLORS	AA TUXEDO BLACK	CC ERMINE WHITE	DD GROTTO BLUE	EE FATHOM BLUE	FF ISLAND TEAL	GG ASH GOLD	HH GRECIAN GREEN	KK TRIPOLI TURQUOISE	LL TEAL BLUE	NN CORDOVAN MAROON	PP SEAFROST GREEN	RR MATADOR RED	TT PALOMINO IVORY	VV SEQUOIA GREEN	YY BUTTERNUT YELLOW	GT ASH GOLD/PALOMINO IVORY	LF TEAL BLUE/ISLAND TEAL
SPORT COUPE & CONVERTIBLE (Standard Interior) COUPE & CONVERTIBLE (with Strato-bucket Seats†)	V I N Y L	BLACK	•	•	•	•	•	•	•	•	•	•	•	•	•	•			
		BLUE (with Strato-bucket Seats Only)	•	•	•	•				•									
		GOLD	•	•				•					•	•	•	•			
		PARCHMENT/BLACK (Exc. Conv. Std. Seat)	•	•	•	•	•	•	•	•		•	•	•	•	•			
		TEAL	•	•		•	•			•			•						•
		RED (Exc. Cpe. with Std. Seat)	•	•					•				•						

†Optional at Extra Cost. §Second color on instrument panel, carpet and steering wheel.

SS 396 color and trim choices for 1968.

The 1968 Chevelle SS 396 sport coupe weighed 3,500 pounds and sold for $3,249.

1968 Chevelle 300 two-door.

CHAPTER SIX
One Of A Kind

When the 1969 Chevelle made its debut on September 26, 1968, it (like the other 1969 Chevrolet models) could practically be tailor-built to the owner's individual tastes. Exclusive options such as computer-selected springs for a better ride, jet stream headlight washers for better illumination in bad weather and night driving, wider wheels to improve vehicle handling and a liquid chain to increase rear tire traction on icy roads were just a few of the available extras to help make the 1969 Chevelle just a little more fun to own. E. M. Estes, then general manager of Chevrolet, stated that with all the various trim options and packages available, over 300 varieties of Chevelle could be produced.

A total of fourteen models was on the market for 1969. The most expensive model was the nine-passenger Concours estate wagon selling for $3,602. At the other end of the ladder was the 300 DeLuxe Coupe for $2,883. The entire Chevelle 300 line was discontinued leaving the 300 DeLuxe coupe, sedan and hardtop coupe as the economy models. The Nomad wagon was placed in the same category with

Now in its second year of production was this 1969 Concours four-door sport sedan. The special trim made it one of the most elegant mid-size cars on the road. The sub-series Concours sport sedan was discontinued at the end of the model run.

the 300 DeLuxe, and was available only as a six-passenger, Model 13235, for $3,094, or Model 13236 if the Dual-Action tailgate was ordered, for $3,136.

The SS 396 was truly not a model unto itself as had been the case in the previous years but was now classed as an option available for Malibu sport coupe, convertible, 300 sport coupe and coupe using the 396 ci engine, special wheels, a more ornate side-panel stripe and the distinctive SS hood louvers. This entire package sold for $350. So, basically, the 300 DeLuxe and Malibu were the two Chevelle models with a sub-series of SS 396 cars.

The 1969 models continued using the two wheelbases they began with in 1968: 112 and 116 inches.

The engine and transmissions that were available are listed in this chapter. The overdrive was no longer produced.

The tire size for all regular models in 1969 was 7.35x14. Those cars equipped with the SS 396 package required F70x14 white-lettered tires.

Chevelle saw a production run for 1969 that was even healthier than the year before. A total of 453,000

vehicles was produced. Of these, 31,000 came as 300 DeLuxe V-8s and 11,000 were built with six-cylinder engines. The larger number came in the Malibu line, with 343,600 V-8s and 23,500 sixes. As for wagon production, 38,500 were powered with V-8 powerplants leaving 7,400 to the six-cylinder operation.

Some facelifting was about all that was in store for the 1969 cars. The new look included a new blacked-out grille and taillights that were more rectangular, placed farther up on the quarter panel rear cap. The coupe and convertible models went along with most other GM models by using Vista-Ventilation, which simply meant the windwings were now history. To me this was one of the poorest moves ever made, but I guess GM figured it was an ideal way to introduce more people to air-conditioned cars.

Cars wearing the 396 emblem also came with power disc brakes as standard equipment. On the inside the SS emblem appeared on the dashboard and the steering wheel.

Bucket seats again were popular options, especially for the younger buyers. If the car came with a bench

Still holding its popularity was the 1969 Malibu convertible. It weighed 3,300 pounds and sold for $3,225.

A front view of the SS 396 showing the black-accented grille.

The left rear quarter view of the 1969 Malibu Concours sport sedan. The trim below the rear deck was done in stainless to help distinguish it from regular Malibu sport sedans.

seat and an automatic, the gear selector was on the steering column; if buckets were ordered, the selector was placed in the front console. All "special three-speed" and four-speed units came with a floor-mounted shift, with or without the console. For the first time, all units with a manual transmission offered a safety starter switch, which prevented the car from starting without having the clutch depressed.

Chevrolet preferred to down-play any type of planned racing during the 1969 model run for Chevelle, but here and there some small events did take place. The 1969 SS 396 could do a quarter mile in 15.4 seconds. The really big news, however, was the few Chevelles that were equipped with the Corvette 425 hp aluminum-head 427 engine. How many were actually produced is not certain but authorities feel it safe to say approximately 500 were built. Wouldn't it be great to have one of these rare beauties today!

Probably it was a good move that the 396 package was available in more than just the SS 396 coupe and convertibles, as it gave people a chance to own these neat cars who didn't wish to tie up additional capital in just a fancier body shell. Since Chevrolet offered it as an option under RPO Z 25, there were 86,307 Chevelles carrying this kit. The rarest of all these models is the SS 396 Malibu DeLuxe coupe. From the research I've been able to do, fewer than 1,000 were produced. I wonder how many are with us today!

A well-designed intake flushed the rocker panels while a constant flow of air removed the moisture. Special outlets drained at the rear of the rocker panels allowing the free flow of air and water.

Special SS 396 nameplate mounted on the front right fender.

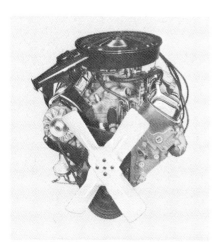

Some bright accents on the SS 396 engine.

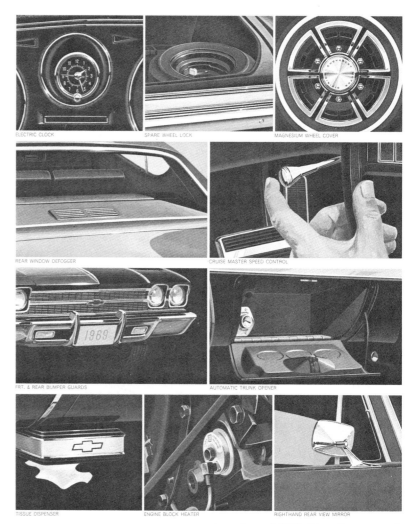

A variety of 1969 Chevelle custom features that all helped one to individualize his or her car.

A rear view showing the Dual-Action tailgate for the 1969 Concours estate wagon. One photo shows it dropped down ready for a picnic; the other displays the tailgate swung out. This model, now in nine-passenger style, came with the rear seat facing the opposite direction. The car was the most expensive model built in the Chevelle line and sold for $3,602. The six-passenger model sold for $3,489.

This is the plush interior of the Concours estate wagon for 1969 done with long-wearing vinyl upholstery, deep twist carpeting, and a new instrument cluster with wood-grain accents.

The lowest-priced Chevelle four-door sedan for 1969 was this 300 DeLuxe weighing 3,230 pounds and selling for $2,912.

Sport Wheels

Mag-Spoke Wheel Cover

This 1969 Malibu sport coupe came with a much larger stainless rocker molding than the model had offered in previous years. The unit sold for $3,025 when equipped with the 307 ci V-8 engine.

Hub Cap and Trim Rings

A sampling of special wheel decor that was available at extra cost on 1969 Chevelles. Top photo shows the Sport wheel package available for the SS 396 cars. Middle photo displays the mag spoke wheel cover; the bottom photo shows the plain hubcap and trim ring arrangement.

This totally original 1969 Malibu sport coupe is owned by a friend of our family, Alma Smith. The car has over 100,000 miles but still runs like new.

A close-up view of the 1969 Malibu grille and placement of the fender marker designating that this vehicle is equipped with a 307 ci engine.

The deluxe wheel cover used on most 1969 Chevelles.

The block-letter Malibu identification was placed on the rear quarter panels next to the red side-maker lights for 1969 models.

The stainless rocker molding was wider than in previous years. It also extended into the lower rear quarter panel.

A 1969 Malibu sport sedan (in its second year using this body style) weighed 3,340 pounds in base form, and sold for $2,745 when equipped with the 307 ci V-8 powerplant. The wheelbase was 116 inches on the four-door car.

The 396 ci Turbo-Jet V-8 developed 350 hp.

ENGINE	TRANSMISSION	REAR AXLE RATIO MODEL APPLICATION	REAR AXLE RATIO							
			Without Air Conditioning				With Air Conditioning			
			Standard	Economy†	Performance†	Special†	Standard	Economy†	Performance†	Special
STANDARD SIX 140-HP TURBO-THRIFT 230 230-CU.-IN. SIX	3-Speed (2.85:1 Low) / Special 3-Speed (3.03:1 Low)	All models	3.08:1		3.36:1		3.36:1		3.55:1	
	Powerglide	All models	3.08:1	2.73:1	3.36:1		3.36:1	3.08:1	3.55:1	
	Turbo Hydra-Matic	All models	2.73:1	2.56:1	3.08:1	3.36:1	3.08:1	2.73:1	3.36:1	
RPO L22 155-HP TURBO-THRIFT 250 250-CU.-IN. SIX	3-Speed (2.85:1 Low) / Special 3-Speed (3.03:1 Low)	All models	3.08:1	2.73:1	3.36:1		3.36:1	3.08:1	3.55:1	
	Powerglide	All models	3.08:1	2.73:1	3.36:1	3.55:1	3.36:1	3.08:1	3.55:1	
	Turbo Hydra-Matic	All models	2.73:1	2.56:1	3.08:1	3.36:1	3.08:1	2.73:1	3.36:1	
STANDARD V8 200-HP TURBO-FIRE 307 307-CU.-IN. V8	3-Speed (2.85:1 Low) / Special 3-Speed (3.03:1 Low)	All models	3.08:1	2.73:1	3.36:1		3.36:1	3.08:1	3.55:1	
	4-Speed (2.85:1 Low)	All models	3.36:1	3.08:1	3.55:1		3.36:1	3.08:1	3.55:1	
	Powerglide	All models	3.08:1	2.73:1	3.36:1	3.55:1	3.36:1	3.08:1	3.55:1	
	Turbo Hydra-Matic	All models	2.73:1	2.56:1	3.08:1	3.36:1	3.08:1	2.73:1	3.36:1	
RPO LM1 255-HP TURBO-FIRE 350 350-CU.-IN. V8	Special 3-Speed (2.42:1 Low) / 4-Speed (2.52:1 Low)	All models	3.31:1	3.07:1	3.55:1		3.31:1	3.07:1	3.55:1	
	Powerglide	All models	2.73:1	2.56:1	3.08:1	3.36:1	2.73:1	2.56:1	3.08:1	3.36:1
	Turbo Hydra-Matic	All models	2.56:1			3.36:1 / 3.08:1	2.56:1			3.36:1 / 3.08:1
RPO L48 300-HP TURBO-FIRE 350 350-CU.-IN. V8	Special 3-Speed (2.42:1 Low) / 4-Speed (2.52:1 Low)	All models	3.31:1	3.07:1	3.55:1		3.31:1	3.07:1	3.55:1	
	Powerglide	All models	2.73:1	2.56:1	3.08:1	3.36:1	2.73:1	2.56:1	3.08:1	3.36:1
	Turbo Hydra-Matic	All models	2.56:1			3.08:1 / 3.36:1	2.56:1			3.08:1 / 3.36:1
325-HP TURBO-JET 396 396-CU.-IN. V8 INCLUDED WITH SS 396 EQUIPMENT (RPO Z25)	Special 3-Speed (2.42:1 Low)	All models	3.31:1	3.07:1	3.55:1	3.73:1* / 4.10:1*	3.31:1	3.07:1	3.55:1	3.73:1
	4-Speed (2.52:1 Low)	All models	3.55:1	3.31:1	3.73:1	3.07:1 / 4.10:1*	3.55:1	3.31:1	3.73:1	3.07:1
	Turbo Hydra-Matic	All models	3.31:1	3.07:1		2.73:1	3.31:1	3.07:1		2.73:1
RPO L34 350-HP TURBO-JET 396 396-CU.-IN. V8	Special 3-Speed (2.42:1 Low) / 4-Speed (2.52:1 Low)	All models	3.55:1	3.31:1	3.73:1*	4.10:1*	3.55:1	3.31:1	3.73:1*	
AVAILABLE WITH SS 396 EQUIPMENT (RPO Z25) ONLY	4-Speed (2.20:1 Low) / Turbo Hydra-Matic	All models	3.55:1	3.31:1	3.73:1*	3.07:1 / 4.10:1*	3.55:1	3.31:1	3.73:1*	3.07:1

Note: Positraction rear axle available in all axle ratios. †Available at extra cost—see Options and Prices section. *Available as Positraction axle only.

1969 Chevelle power teams.

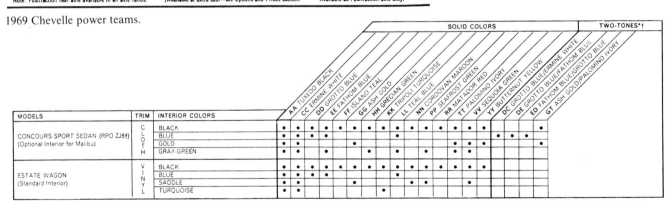

Concours estate wagon and Concours sport sedan colors and trim for 1969.

*Two-Tones Not Available on Convertible.

1969 SS 396 color and trim choices.

†Optional at Extra Cost. §Second color on instrument panel, carpet and steering wheel.

CHAPTER SEVEN
Two Cars For All Seasons

Beginning with (the) 1970 there was not only the Chevelle, but also the new prestige car introduced by Chevrolet on September 18, 1969, the Monte Carlo.

For 1970 the number of models dwindled in the Chevelle line. Gone was the 300 DeLuxe series; replacing it was the Chevelle, technically called the 133 series if equipped with a six-cylinder engine or 134 series if the V-8 powerplant was used. It came as a two-door sport coupe and four-door sedan; its equivalent in the wagon line was the two-seat six-passenger Nomad known as Model 13236.

All models continued on the same two wheelbases used since this arrangement was begun in 1968. The overall length of the sport sedan and sedan was 201.9 inches. The sport coupe and convertible came with 197.2-inch overall length, and the wagons had an overall length of 206.5 inches.

For the speed enthusiast, there was big news in the engine compartment. There, by order, could be the new 454 ci monster that developed 450 hp at 5600 rpm. It was technically referred to as the LS-6 option. This engine has been rated as one of the all-time great

A 1970 SS 396 sport coupe with the complete 396 sport package. This example is displayed with the blacked-out grille, Rally wheels and hood-cowl induction (at the base of the hood, the dome opened to allow high-pressure air from around the windshield to come into the carburetor). This model also came with the optional 454 ci engine. Sitting in this style could have run over $4,500 with all the trimmings.

engines by noted race performers and enthusiasts. This engine in a sport coupe was clocked at 108.77 mph in 13.44 seconds in the quarter mile. The engine package ranged in price from $263.30 for just the 454 engine to $503.45 including the various trim options. Those units that were on the street saw very few that could hold a candle to it. Possibly only a well-tuned Hemi could come close. The high-compression heads (11.25:1) and a very strong solid-lifter camshaft were what made the great performance of these Chevelles. However, the majority of these 1970 models wearing the SS 454 badge used a 454 rated at 360 hp with 10.25:1 heads. Needless to say, both engines required premium fuel.

The 396 engine, which had made history with Chevrolet the past few seasons, actually increased to 402 ci even though the factory continued to rate it as a 396 block. Possibly, it was felt it would be too confusing to the general public to make another change. All 1970 Chevrolet muscle engines used "slim-line" spark plugs.

With the SS 396 came the F-41 suspension (stiffer springs, firmer shocks and a rear antiroll bar), power-assisted front disc brakes, seven-inch wheels and F-70 belted-bias tires. The transmission was either the close-ratio four-speed manual or Turbo Hydra-matic.

The tire sizes for these models were as follows: Six-cylinder cars came with E-78x14 tires. The V-8 models came with F-78x14s or wide-oval F-70x14 white-lettered tires with 14x7 wheels for the street machines.

The Malibu series continued to be the most popular line with the SS 396s and 454s classed as a sub-series. Incidentally the SS again became available only on the sport coupe and convertible.

A nice facelift for the year gave the cars a look of class. The fender bulge begun on the 1969 Chevrolet was now a part of the Chevelle, and a new squared-off front end gave that extra bit of distinction.

Beginning in 1970 the SS Chevelle was the first SS to carry a dash panel different from other Chevelles. Its panel resembled the new Monte Carlo a great deal, with round gauges in front of the driver. On the exterior, little items made quite a difference in the overall

A real "mean" automobile was this 1970 SS 396 convertible. The 396 option cost an additional $445.55. Besides this engine the 454 ci could be ordered for $503.45, which also included the complete SS package of special domed hood, suspension, black-painted grille and 14x7 sport wheels, just to mention a few of the frills.

Attracting more buyers of convertibles than the SS 396 version was the plain Malibu convertible, Model 13667. I'm sure the reason for its being more in demand was the price of $3,350.

package. They included a special domed hood with its chrome release attachments, black rear bumper insert with the SS emblem, dual chrome exhaust tips, black-accented grille with the familiar SS emblem. And, to let the public know what you were driving, SS 396 or SS 454 emblems were neatly placed on the front fenders. Wheelhouse moldings helped to keep the nicks from appearing on the body, and gave it a little more class. An additional way to help distinguish regular Chevelles from SS models is to remember that regular models came with amber parking lenses while the Super Sports carried clear lenses for their parking-light covers.

Production of the 1970 Chevelles amounted to 354,855 units with 53,599 carrying the 396 engine and 3,773 using the 454 block.

The 1970 Monte Carlo made its debut at Chevrolet dealerships on September 18, 1969. It was offered as a personal luxury car and came in only one body style, sport coupe. This model had the longest hood ever produced on any Chevrolet: six feet. The car came on a 116-inch wheelbase.

I remember falling in love the minute I first set eyes on it. A Monte Carlo was being detailed in the new car department of our local dealership in late August of 1969. The fever began to mount then and has never subsided. My problem was that I had just purchased a new Volkswagen six months before and wondered how I was going to dispose of it. My next-door neighbor was very glad to help me out, so I got the nicely equipped Gobi Beige coupe which is shown in this book. Today it has just 34,000 miles on it.

The 1970 accessory catalog for Chevelle and Monte Carlo shows (on page six) the Monte Carlo built as a convertible, which certainly would be a collectable today. Unfortunately, there never was even one built. The sport coupe was available as the SS 454 in addition to the regular Monte Carlo. The only exterior difference between the regular Monte Carlo and the SS 454 was the SS 454 nameplate on the lower front fender. This car was a real treat.

A 1970 Monte Carlo with the 454 engine was road tested shortly after its debut, by *Car Life.* This fierce machine climbed to 132 mph before being backed off.

The most popular wagon Chevelle offered for 1970 was this Concours six-passenger, Model 13636. It weighed 3,794 pounds and had a price tag of $3,556. The nine-passenger version cost an additional $113.

It did 0-60 in just over seven seconds. That's moving!

The Monte Carlo 454 chassis differed slightly from regular models by using heavy-duty shocks with an automatic level control that was built into the self-regulating rear air devices. This attractive car actually didn't resemble any other Chevrolet all that much, and yet you knew it was a Chevrolet. The only place on the car where the name Chevrolet appeared was on the panel beneath the trunk where the nameplate was mounted, saying "Monte Carlo by Chevrolet."

In many respects the Monte Carlo and Chevelle were blood brothers under the skin. Both cars used the Fisher A-body structure, and some components were interchangeable between them—such as the deck lid and winshield. The Monte Carlo wheelbase was the same as that of Chevelle sedans and wagons, 116 inches. The roofline gave a more classic touch than that of the Chevelle since its buyer was looking for a car with that type of personal appeal. The man mainly responsible for the patrician lines of the Monte Carlo was the chief designer at Chevrolet during this time, David Holls. Holls was an authority on the classic styling of the thirties. We all thank him for his great contribution to a refreshing design that is improving with age.

Most Monte Carlos came with Turbo Hydra-matic drive; few were produced as sticks. I nearly purchased a plain Monte Carlo a few years ago simply because of the strange arrangement of having a stick transmission. Besides a three-speed, a four-speed setup also was available on special order. I feel quite certain that at least 100 Monte Carlos were built using the 454 ci with four-speed transmission. The standard Monte Carlo engine was the 350 V-8. Optional was the "400" V-8.

There appears to be some confusion as to the different types of 454 V-8 that were available. All the 454s built weren't equipped as 360 hp units. There was also the regular-production option 215 SS powerplant. The optional LS6 454, which developed 450 hp, was used in some Chevelles and in a few Monte Carlos. At least one Monte Carlo saw daylight with the LS5 454 engine, which developed 390 hp. The M 20 wide-ratio four-speed gearbox was offered with the 400 V-8 Monte

Classic, simple lines are shown in this 1970 Monte Carlo coupe. It sports the not-too-often-seen fender skirts which I say are a nuisance but a must.

This is the 1970 Monte Carlo SS 454 which was produced in a limited supply. Note the 454 emblem on the rocker molding by the front right fender. This was the only telling point until you raised the hood.

Carlo, and could be specially ordered for the SS 454. The M 21 close-ratio 2.20:1 low box was a Chevelle SS 454 option that was also placed in a few Monte Carlos.

The plants that began assembling Monte Carlos were afflicted by strikes in the very first days of production. This kept us from seeing as many Monte Carlos as dealers and myself would have liked to see on the road.

Only 3,823 SS 454 Monte Carlos were produced for 1970. The regular Monte Carlos had a production run of 130,657.

The day I took delivery of my new Monte Carlo, March 18, 1970, the car cost $4,346. I said, "This is terrible, I'll never spend that much again for a new car." Unfortunately, I probably won't be able to keep my vow, with prices as they are today.

This sharp Cranberry Red 1970 SS 454 Monte Carlo belongs to Tom Parsons of California. The front view shows the single headlights that preserve the model's simplicity. The center grille emblem carries the Roman numerals MCMLXX, a subtle appointment to let you know it's a 1970. Note the license plate.

The SS 454 identification plate on Tom Parsons' 1970 Monte Carlo.

Some detailed views of the 1970 Chevrolet Monte Carlo and its special features.

After thirteen years of use Tom Parsons'
454 is still clean.

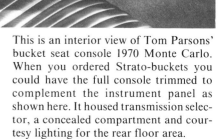

A rear-quarter view of a 1970 Monte
Carlo at the Chevrolet zone office in
Detroit. One thing is wrong in this photo:
The car sports both the Corvette-style
wire wheel covers and skirts. This option
doesn't work. I know—I tried it. The skirt
rubs on the center of the cover due to its
pointed flare.

This is an interior view of Tom Parsons'
bucket seat console 1970 Monte Carlo.
When you ordered Strato-buckets you
could have the full console trimmed to
complement the instrument panel as
shown here. It housed transmission selector, a concealed compartment and courtesy lighting for the rear floor area.

A view of a 396 V-8 engine as displayed in
a 1970 Super Sport that is owned by Len
Cormier, of Cormier Chevrolet Company
in Long Beach, California.

An interior view of a 1970 Super Sport coupe with its four-on-the-floor shift mechanism and bench seat. The round dash gauges made it appear much like the new Monte Carlo.

A close-up view of the rear bumper compartment of a 1970 Super Sport. The SS emblem was neatly placed in the blacked-out portion of the bumper. Chromed exhaust tips were part of the Super Sport package.

The Super Sport Rally wheel for 1970 was mounted on this G70x14 tire. The SS 396 emblems were mounted on both lower front fenders to help distinguish them from regular 1970 Chevelles.

A feature only for the Super Sport models was the chromed hood release attachments as seen on this 1970 sport coupe.

Note the special domed hood with cowl induction vent and the cowl induction nameplate mounted on each side of the raised portion of this 1970 Super Sport coupe.

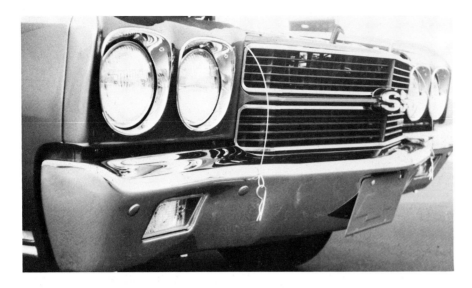

This photo of a 1970 Chevelle wearing its SS badge in the center of the grille shows the hood attachments released. This was the final year for Chevelles to use the quad headlamps. The parking lamps were mounted at the outer portion of the bumper similar to the 1968 lens models. Chevelle had clear lenses; Malibu had amber lenses.

Note the similarity between this rear bumper on a regular 1970 Chevelle and that on the 1970 Super Sport. This unit carries the accessory bumper guards, which sold for $11.25 per pair. The part number was 993805 for the front units and 993827 for the rear ones.

Looking quite similar to the 1970 Super Sport is this regular 1970 Malibu front end. It features a chromed grille rather than the blacked-out version as seen on the Super Sport model. This example carries a 350 ci engine, as designated on the front fender. The fender openings also do not carry the stainless molding as seen on Super Sport models.

The standard hubcap used for all 1970 Chevelles except for the Super Sport cars.

A popular car with almost everyone was this 1970 Malibu sport coupe. It sold for $3,150 when equipped with the standard V-8 engine, and weighed 3,307. This 1970 Chevelle Malibu coupe is owned by Richard and Mary Lou Eckert of California. The car has well over 100,000 miles.

The uncluttered appearance of the front end on the 1970 Monte Carlo has always made it a model with appeal among Chevrolet collectors. The hood ornament on this unit should be for a 1971—I know because it's my car and back in 1971 I upgraded it a year.

A view of the 1970 Monte Carlo with fender skirts. This accessory, which not too many came equipped with, cost the buyer an additional $31.80. The pinstripe was not a Monte Carlo feature but a little treat I gave it after a trip East in 1970.

Here are the deluxe wheel covers most 1970 Chevelles came equipped with. The dealer price for this accessory was $22.75 per set of four. The part number was 993918.

A rear view of the 1970 personalized luxury Monte Carlo. The bumper-guard equipment was an accessory for the year. Like the skirts, it was not seen on many cars. The guards sold for the same price of $11.75 per pair as on the Chevelle.

This is a view of the 350 ci engine which both my 1970 Monte Carlos are equipped with. Note the huge shroud over the fan area. Basically, being so similar to the Chevelle, the Monte Carlo needed something to fill this large area under the six-foot-long hood. Also note air conditioning compressor mounted to the right.

Fore and aft views of my 1970 Monte Carlos. Both cars are equipped just about the same, except the Shadow Grey one is minus the vinyl top which makes it look plainer.

The standard wheel cover used on Monte Carlo for 1970 through 1972 models.

This is the correct hood ornament for 1970 Monte Carlos. It is just the basic, simple chrome spear.

	3-Speed	4-Speed	Powerglide	Turbo Hydra-matic
Standard Engines				
155-hp Turbo-Thrift 250 Six	•		•	•
200-hp Turbo-Fire 307 V8	•	•	•	•
Extra-Cost Engines				
250-hp Turbo-Fire 350 V8	•	•	•	•
300-hp Turbo-Fire 350 V8		•	•	•
330-hp Turbo-Jet 400 V8		•		•
SS Engines				
350-hp Turbo-Jet 396 V8		•		•
360-hp Turbo-Jet 454 V8		•		•

1970 Chevelle power teams.

	3-Speed	4-Speed	Power-glide	Turbo Hydra-matic
250-hp Turbo-Fire 350 V8*	*	•	•	•
300-hp Turbo-Fire 350 V8		•	•	•
265-hp Turbo-Fire 400 V8		•		•
330-hp Turbo-Jet 400 V8		•		•
360-hp Turbo-Jet 454 V8†				•

*Standard
†For Monte Carlo SS only.

Features of the 1970 Chevelle.

Your Chevrolet Monte Carlo checklist.
Use this checklist to tailor Monte Carlo to your tastes. Then take it to your Chevrolet dealer with questions on price and model/equipment availability.

Interiors (extra cost)
- ☐ All-vinyl Strato-bucket seats
- ☐ Black vinyl and custom knit nylon Strato-bucket seats

Engines
- ☐ 250-hp Turbo-Fire 350 V8 (standard)
- ☐ 300-hp Turbo-Fire 350 V8
- ☐ 265-hp Turbo-Fire 400 V8
- ☐ 330-hp Turbo-Jet 400 V8
- ☐ 360-hp Turbo-Jet 454 V8 (SS only)

Transmissions
- ☐ 3-Speed fully synchronized (standard with 250-hp V8)
- ☐ 4-Speed fully synchronized
- ☐ Powerglide automatic
- ☐ Turbo Hydra-matic

Popular extras
- ☐ Monte Carlo SS
- ☐ Variable-ratio power steering
- ☐ Power door locks
- ☐ Automatic seat back release
- ☐ Finger-tip wiper control
- ☐ Rear fender skirts
- ☐ Power trunk release
- ☐ Stereo tape system

Magic-Mirror acrylic lacquer finishes
- ☐ Gobi Beige
- ☐ Tuxedo Black
- ☐ Astro Blue
- ☐ Fathom Blue
- ☐ Black Cherry
- ☐ Desert Sand
- ☐ Autumn Gold
- ☐ Champagne Gold
- ☐ Forest Green
- ☐ Cranberry Red
- ☐ Cortez Silver
- ☐ Shadow Gray
- ☐ Misty Turquoise
- ☐ Classic White
- ☐ Green Mist

Chevelle options for 1970.

CHAPTER EIGHT
Return To Single Headlights

The 1971 Chevelle offered pretty much the same package as in 1970. The Chevelle's only noticeable differences were in the return to single headlights and in the round taillights mounted to each bumper tip. The number of models amounted to fourteen, including the mid-season offering of the Heavy Chevy, which was the economical way of having a Super Sport without quite as much trim. The Heavy Chevy CRPO 4 F 37 was considered a companion model to the Nova Rally. It wore the Super Sport domed head with lock pins, Rally wheels in the 14x6 size, a blacked-out grille and the decal stripes. You could easily identify this model by the Heavy Chevy lettering on the front fenders and at the rear of the car. A customer had the choice of engines ranging from the 307 Turbo-Fire V-8 to the 400 Turbo-Jet. The cowl induction was an available option minus the stripe.

Not shown on availability charts but still available was the 454 LS-6. This engine was the only one with a 9.0:1 compression ratio. The horsepower was rated at 435. The plain Chevelle SS came with a 245 or 270 hp Turbo-Fire 350 V-8 or a 300 hp Turbo-Jet 400 V-8. With

A true muscle car was the 1971 SS sport coupe. The special Sport wheels were standard equipment on this and Heavy Chevy models.

This 1971 Chevelle Malibu sport coupe sported the optional custom simulated wire wheel covers (RPO PO2) for $82 per set of four. This was Model 13637. It weighed 3,286 pounds and sold for $3,316.

so many engines available it was extremely difficult for customers to know what to order, and for sales personnel to advise a customer what package would be most appropriate for him. Many dealers simply advised customers who wished a high-performance vehicle to take the 454 V-8 and forget the extra-cost options because that might mean they'd wait months for delivery or never receive the car at all.

Even fewer SS Chevelles saw daylight in 1971. With only 19,293 of these units produced it was perhaps a telling sign that the public wasn't quite as interested in the high-performance cars as it once was. Their scarcity makes them rather difficult to locate today. If you own one, feel lucky that you've got one of the last true muscle cars.

Monte Carlo was introduced for 1971 as practically the same car as in 1970. The facelift featured a grille with finely textured horizontal bars, a hood emblem stating Monte Carlo, rectangular parking lights mounted in the bumper, a crest concealing the trunk key opening and different wheel covers if you chose the deluxe discs. For those desiring the Monte Carlo

454 a few additional items helped distinguish it from its less fancy brother: special black-accented rear panels beneath the deck lid, an SS emblem mounted on the lower right with the series script, the black accent panel typical of other Chevrolet SS models, dual chromed exhaust tips, and 15x7 Rally wheels. These items were all classed as standard equipment.

For the interior a four-spoke steering wheel, Strato-bucket front seats and an AM-FM stereo tape unit were all considered to be desirable options to make your Monte Carlo a pleasure to drive. Available only on the 454 models were the fashionable "soft knobs" for the instrument panel buttons.

Almost all Monte Carlos came with Turbo Hydra-matic as the recommended option. However, a few did slip through with the three-speed, and with the 454 engine some were seen on special order to have a four-speed manual transmission. Also, a few came with the LS-6 option of the 454 engine.

Some of the special chassis parts for 1971 SS Monte Carlos were heavier shocks with the Automatic Level Control rear air bar and heavy-duty springs front and

Views of the remaining Malibu line for 1971. In the foreground sits a Malibu four-door sedan, Model 13699, which sold for $3,282. Behind it to the left is the Malibu sport sedan, Model 13639, with a price tag of $3,388. To the right is the Malibu convertible, Model 13667, which cost $3,590.

64

rear with double-duty front and rear stabilizers.

Sales of the SS Monte Carlo continued to dwindle just as was happening in the Chevelle SS camp for 1971. Only 1,919 SS Monte Carlos were built for the entire model run. Very little was told about it in sales brochures and virtually no advertising appeared in magazines. Production figures for regular 1971 Monte Carlos are not currently available from Chevrolet.

The quality of handling was quite similar in each class, whether one compared a regular Malibu coupe to the Monte Carlo coupe or whether a Chevelle SS Turbo-Fire 350 V-8 was put up against a Monte Carlo with a big-block.

For me to even pick a Chevrolet apart is the crime of the week, but I must be truly honest about it. I've never felt either of these models had the riding qualities that every Chevrolet enthusiast has tried to make the public believe they had. When my 1968 Chevelle or 1970 Monte Carlo has six passengers it rides well; otherwise, I've always felt neither holds the road as the salesmen were trying to tell us they did. The handling is a bit sloppy, especially in the rear end.

A well-balanced rear view on the 1971 Monte Carlo. Only change seen here was a crest over the trunk-locking device.

A rear view showing off the sporting stripes and new, round taillights of the 1971 SS model.

This was Chevelle's most expensive car for 1971. It's the Concours estate wagon for eight passengers. It weighed 3,928 pounds and sold for $3,962.

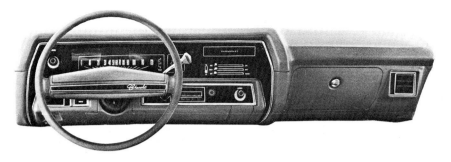

The 1971 Chevelle dashboard had all controls neatly arranged for the driver.

The attractive fender skirts sold for an additional $31.60. They were the same style through 1972.

An interior view of the Malibu showing its optional all-vinyl interior for 1971.

Special custom wire wheel covers used during the three-year run of this model.

There was only a slight difference between the regular Monte Carlo coupe and this SS model: This unit wears the special Rally wheels (RPO ZJ7) as standard equipment. The SS 454 can be identified on the lower right front fender. Heavy-duty springs were required on this 365 hp Turbo-Jet 454 V-8.

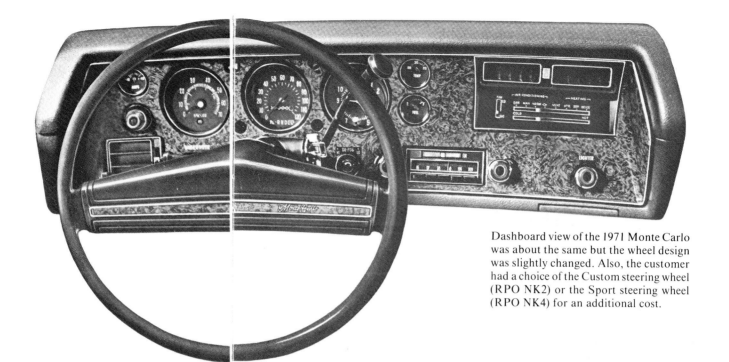

Dashboard view of the 1971 Monte Carlo was about the same but the wheel design was slightly changed. Also, the customer had a choice of the Custom steering wheel (RPO NK2) or the Sport steering wheel (RPO NK4) for an additional cost.

The taillamps were slightly changed with small bars placed both vertically and horizontally in the lens for the 1971 cars.

This was the DeLuxe wheel disc used on the 1971 Monte Carlo.

The deluxe wheel discs were used on all Chevelle models as an option. Most customers ordered them.

The round taillamps in the oval openings were first seen on the 1971 Chevelles. This example belongs to Vic and Rosemary Korth.

The 1971 front end saw the return to single headlamps. Parking lamps and side-marker lamps were incorporated into one unit for the first time.

This well-kept 1971 Monte Carlo is owned by Josephine Moran of California. The lady to her left is my mother, Mrs. Moloney.

The Malibu and engine-size identification nameplates were mounted on the lower portion of both front fenders for the 1971 models.

The clean lines of the front end, the horizontal grille bars and the oval hood emblem mark this as a 1971 Monte Carlo.

The Rally Sport magnesium wheel covers sold for $56.85 per set of four on both Chevelles and Monte Carlos during the 1970-72 era.

Chevelle Interior Features	Chevelle	Malibu	SS
Convenient T-handle parking brake release	•	•	•
Courtesy lights under instrument panel (Convertible only)		•	•
Suspended accelerator pedal	•	•	•
Foot-operated parking brake	•	•	•
Day-night rearview mirror	•	•	•
Scuff-resistant plastic cowl side panels	•	•	•
Armrests front and rear	•	•	•
Forward-mounted front door lock buttons	•	•	•
Pattern cloth and vinyl interior trim (except Convertible)	•	•	
All-vinyl interior trim (standard on Convertible)	EC	EC	EC
All-vinyl Strato-bucket seats (Sport Coupe and Convertible only)		EC	EC
Color-keyed deep-twist carpeting		•	•
Center dome light (except Convertible)	•	•	•
Vinyl-coated luggage compartment mat		•	•

EC—Extra cost

Chevelle interior features for 1971.

Chevelle and Malibu Interior Features	Chevelle	Malibu	SS
Oval steering wheel	•	•	
Black steering wheel and column with SS emblem			•
Bright instrument cluster outline molding	•	•	
Special black-finish instrument panel and cluster			•
Astro Ventilation vent-ports	(a)	(b)	•
Automatic ignition key alarm	•	•	•
Illuminated heater control panel	•	•	•
Glove compartment lock		•	•
Glove compartment light		•	•
Cigarette lighter	•	•	•
Oil pressure, temperature, and generator warning lights	•	•	•
Parking brake and brake system warning light	•	•	•
Color-keyed turn signal and shift lever knobs	•	•	•
Padded instrument panel and sun visors	•	•	•

(a) Sport Coupe only   (b) Sport Coupe and Convertible only

1971 interior features of Chevelles and Malibus.

model	seat style	Black cloth	Black vinyl	Dark Blue cloth	Dark Jade cloth	Dark Jade vinyl	Saddle vinyl	Sandalwood cloth
Coupe — conventional	conventional	708		728	734			717
Coupe — Strato-Bucket (RPO A51)	Strato-Bucket (RPO A51)	707	710	727	733	729	723	716

Exterior Colors

Exterior Colors	code	Black	Dark Blue	Dark Jade	Saddle	Sandalwood
Tuxedo Black	19	•	•	•	•	•
Mulsanne Blue	26	•	•			•
Ascot Blue	24	•	•			•
Classic Copper	67	•				•
Placer Gold	53	•			•	•
Lime Green	43	•		•		•
Cottonwood Green	42	•		•		•
Antique Green	49	•		•	•	•
Burnt Orange	62	•				•
Cranberry Red	75	•				•
Rosewood Metallic	78	•				•
Sandalwood	61	•		•	•	•
Nevada Silver	13	•	•			•
Antique White	11	•	•	•	•	•
Sunflower Yellow	52	•		•		•

two tone combinations

lower color	code	upper color	code	Black	Dark Blue	Dark Jade	Saddle	Sandalwood
Mulsanne Blue	26	Antique White	11	•				•
Placer Gold	53	Antique White	11	•	•		•	•
Antique Green	49	Antique White	11	•		•	•	•
Lime Green	43	Antique White	11	•		•	•	•
Burnt Orange	62	Antique White	11	•				•
Sandalwood	61	Antique White	11	•		•	•	•

models	seat style	Black cloth	Black vinyl	Dark Blue cloth	Dark Blue vinyl	Dark Jade cloth	Dark Jade vinyl	Saddle vinyl	Sandalwood cloth	Sandalwood vinyl
Malibu Sport Coupe — conventional	conventional	704	705	725		730	731	721	718	714
Malibu Sport Coupe — Strato-Bucket (RPO A51)	Strato-Bucket (RPO A51)		706				732	722		715
Malibu Sport Sedan	conventional	704	705	725	726	730	731		718	714
Malibu 4-Door Sedan	conventional	704	705	725		730		721		714
Malibu Convertible — conventional	conventional		705				731	721		
Malibu Convertible — Strato-Bucket (RPO A51)	Strato-Bucket (RPO A51)		706				732	722		
Chevelle Sport Coupe or 4-Door Sedan	conventional	701	703	724		736				

Exterior Colors

Exterior Colors	code	Black	Dark Blue	Dark Jade	Saddle	Sandalwood
Tuxedo Black	19	•	•	•	•	•
Mulsanne Blue	26	•	•			•
Ascot Blue	24	•	•			•
Classic Copper	67	•				•
Placer Gold	53	•			•	•
Lime Green	43	•		•	•	•
Cottonwood Green	42	•		•		•
Antique Green	49	•		•	•	•
Burnt Orange	62	•				•
Cranberry Red	75	•				•
Rosewood Metallic	78	•				•
Sandalwood	61	•		•	•	•
Nevada Silver	13	•	•			•
Antique White	11	•	•	•	•	•
Sunflower Yellow	52	•		•	•	•

two tone combinations

lower color	code	upper color	code	Black	Dark Blue	Dark Jade	Saddle	Sandalwood
Mulsanne Blue	26	Antique White	11	•	•			•
Placer Gold	53	Antique White	11	•			•	•
Antique Green	49	Antique White	11	•		•	•	•
Lime Green	43	Antique White	11	•		•	•	•
Burnt Orange	62	Antique White	11	•				•
Sandalwood	61	Antique White	11	•		•	•	•

Interior trim and exterior color choices for 1971.

Chevelle and Malibu Exterior Features	Chevelle	Malibu	SS
Silver-finish grille	•	•	
Black-accented grille with SS emblem			•
Special domed hood with hood pins			•
Bright grille outline moldings		•	•
Windshield molding	•	•	•
Hood rear edge molding	•	•	•
Hide-A-Way windshield wipers			•
Clear lenses over parking/direction signal lights	•	•	•
Front fender engine emblem—(optional V8, only)	•	•	"454" only
Front fender nameplates—Malibu or SS		•	•
Full door-glass styling (Sport Coupe and Convertible only)	•	•	•
Rectangular outside rearview mirror	•	•	•
Bright roof drip moldings (except Convertible)		•	•
Side marker lights front and rear	•	•	•
Wide body sill moldings		•	
Front and rear wheel opening moldings			•
Hub caps	•	•	
Sport wheels			•
Wide-oval white-lettered tires			•
Rear window molding (except Convertible)	•	•	
Chevelle nameplate on deck lid	•	•	•
Bumper-mounted taillights with silver-finish accents		•	
Bumper-mounted SS emblem			•
Bright twin tailpipe extensions (454 V8 only)			•

Exterior features of 1971 Chevelles and Malibus.

Malibu & Chevelle

Exterior Dimensions	Sport Sedan	Sport Coupe	Convertible	4-Door Sedan
Wheelbase	116.0	112.0	112.0	116.0
Length (overall)	201.5	197.5	197.5	201.5
Width (overall)	75.4	75.4	75.4	75.4
Height (loaded)	53.3	52.7	52.9	53.3
Front tread	60.0	60.0*	60.0*	60.0
Rear tread	59.9	59.9**	59.9**	59.9

*SS: 61.3   **SS: 60.3

Interior Roominess				
Head room—front	38.1	37.5	38.3	38.5
Head room—rear	37.1	36.3	36.9	37.1
Leg room—front	42.8	42.8	42.8	42.7
Leg room—rear	34.9	32.3	32.3	35.0
Hip room—front	59.5	59.7	59.7	59.8
Hip room—rear	59.2	52.9	50.4	59.2
Shoulder room—front	58.4	58.2	58.2	58.2
Shoulder room—rear	57.2	56.9	56.9	57.3
Front entrance height	30.3	29.5	29.5	30.1
Rear entrance height	29.9	—	—	29.5

Luggage Compartment				
Maximum opening width	48.5	48.5	48.5	48.5
Loading height	26.6	25.9	25.9	26.6
Interior length (max.)	49.0	49.0	49.0	49.0
Interior width (max.)	72.0	72.0	72.0	72.0
Interior height (max.)	18.0	18.0	18.0	18.0
Usable luggage space (cu. ft.)	13.5	12.8	9.0	12.8

Glass Area				
Windshield glass area (sq. in.)	1249.6	1208.7	1211.8	1249.6
Rear window glass area (sq. in.)	1032.5	1059.4	539.7	1032.2
Total glass area (sq. in.)	3631.5	3602.1	3011.9	3472.8

Tire Size & Steering Specifications				
Standard tire size—V8		E78 x 14*		
—Six		E78 x 14		
Turning circle—curb-to-curb (ft.)	42.2	42.2		42.2
Turning circle—wall-to-wall (ft.)	45.5	45.3		45.3
Steering ratio—std. (overall)		32.43		
Steering ratio—power (overall)		18.5:1 to 15.06:1		

*SS—F60 x 15

Fuel Capacity & Weight				
Rated fuel tank capacity (gallons)		19		
Curb weight—Six (lbs.)	—	3264/3306†	—	3302/3340†
Curb weight—V8 (lbs.)	3532	3384/3430†	3476	3420/3460†
Shipping weight—Six (lbs.)	—	3164/3208†	—	3204/3242†
Shipping weight—V8 (lbs.)	3434	3286/3332†	3378	3322/3362†

†Chevelle/Malibu

Other features of 1971 Chevelles and Malibus.

Vinyl Roof Cover* Color Choices (RPO C08)

vinyl roof color	code	exterior color availability
Black	BB	all exterior colors
Dark Blue	CC	Tuxedo Black, Mulsanne Blue, Ascot Blue, Nevada Silver or Antique White
Dark Brown	FF	Classic Copper, Burnt Orange, Rosewood Metallic, Sandalwood or Antique White
Dark Green	GG	Tuxedo Black, Lime Green, Cottonwood Green, Antique Green or Antique White
White	AA	all exterior colors

*Optional at extra cost.

Convertible Top Colors: Choice of white or black top available with all exterior colors.

Seat and Shoulder Belt Colors

interior trim color	standard style belts	custom deluxe belts*
Black	Black	Black
Dark Blue	Black	Dark Blue
Dark Jade	Black	Dark Jade
Saddle	Black	Beige
Sandalwood	Black	Sandalwood

*Available at extra cost. Note: Standard seat and shoulder belt buckles black; custom deluxe buckles brush-finished.

Colors for Sport Stripes (RPO D88) and Cowl Induction Hood (RPO ZL2)

exterior color	Sport Coupe without vinyl roof cover		Vinyl Roof Cover or Convertible Top				
	Regular Stripe Color	Optional Stripe Color RPO ZR8	Black vinyl or Convertible	White vinyl or Convertible	Blue vinyl	Brown vinyl	Green vinyl
Tuxedo Black	White		White	White	White		White
Mulsanne Blue	Black	White	Black	White	Black		
Ascot Blue	Black	White	Black	White	Black		
Classic Copper	Black	White	Black	White		Black	
Placer Gold	Black	White	Black	White			
Lime Green	Black	White	Black	White			Black
Cottonwood Green	Black	White	Black	White			Black
Antique Green	Black	White	Black	White			Black
Burnt Orange	Black	White	Black	White		Black	
Cranberry Red	Black	White	Black	White			
Rosewood Metallic	Black	White	Black	White		Black	
Sandalwood	Black	White	Black	White		Black	
Nevada Silver	Black	White	Black	White	Black		
Antique White	Black		Black	Black	Black	Black	Black
Sunflower Yellow	Black	White	Black	White			
two-tone combinations							
Mulsanne Blue/Antique White	White						
Placer Gold/Antique White	White						
Antique Green/Antique White	White						
Lime Green/Antique White	White						
Burnt Orange/White	White						
Sandalwood/Antique White	White						

Chevelle color and trim choices for 1971.

Engines, Transmissions and Axle Ratios   transmissions and rear axle ratios

engines	3-Speed (2.85:1 low)	3-Speed (2.54:1 low)	Special 3-Speed (2.42:1 low)	4-Speed (2.54:1 low)	4-Speed (2.52:1 low)	4-Speed (2.20:1 low)	Powerglide	Turbo Hydra-matic
Standard Six	3.08						3.08	
Standard V8	3.08						3.08	2.73
(RPO L65) 245-hp (165▲) Turbo-Fire 350 V8				3.36				2.56
(RPO L48) 270-hp (175▲) Turbo-Fire 350 V8		3.31		3.31				2.73
(RPO LS3) 300-hp (260▲) Turbo-Jet 400 V8			3.31		3.31			2.73
365-hp (285▲) Turbo-Jet 454 V8 (Available only with SS 454 RPO Z15)						3.31		3.31

▲SAE net (as installed) horsepower

Note: Positraction rear axle available in all axle ratios.

Equipment Included With Optional* V8 Engines

	245-hp (165▲) 350	270-hp (175▲) 350	300-hp (260▲) 400	365-hp (285▲) 454
Heavier duty front and rear shock absorbers			(rear only)	•
Heavier front stabilizer bar				•
Rear suspension frame reinforcement	•	•	•	•
Ring gear—8.875" dia.			•	•
Single exhaust (2½-in. dia.)	•	•		
Dual exhaust (2½-in. dia.)	•	•	•	•
Heavier duty clutch	•	•	•	•
F78 x 14 tires			•	
Wide-oval F60 x 15 white lettered tires with 15 x 7 wheels				•
Heavy-duty battery				•
High-flow air cleaner				•
Higher performance starting motor	•	•	•	•
Special chrome air cleaner cover				•
Deep cover fuel pump and vapor return line to fuel tank				•

▲SAE net (as installed) horsepower

*Optional at extra cost.

1971 engine, transmission and axle ratio features.

Monte Carlo Exterior Features	Monte Carlo Coupe	Monte Carlo SS
Bright precision-cast grille with center crest	•	•
High-output Power-Beam headlights with bright frames	•	•
Rectangular parking/direction signal lights built into front bumper	•	•
Hood windsplit molding with emblem	•	•
Windshield molding	•	•
Hide-A-Way windshield wipers	•	•
Hood rear edge molding	•	•
Full door-glass styling	•	•
Monte Carlo roof rear quarter nameplate	•	
SS 454 nameplate in front fender lower molding		•
Rectangular outside rearview mirror	•	•
Bright roof drip moldings	•	•
Bright door and rear quarter belt moldings	EC	EC
Side marker lights—front and rear	•	•
Black-accented lower body, body sill and fender moldings		•
Bright wheel opening moldings	•	•
Full wheel covers	•	
Wide-rim 15 x 7 Rally Wheels		•
Rear window molding	•	•
Bright rear end panel molding	•	•
Single-unit vertical taillights with bright accents	•	•
Rectangular back-up lights built in rear bumper	•	•
Deck lid crest with integral lock	•	•

EC—Extra cost

Monte Carlo exterior features for 1971.

Monte Carlo Interior Features	Coupe	SS
Oval steering wheel with emblem	•	•
Simulated wood burl accents on instrument panel and steering wheel	•	•
Simulated wood instrument cluster surface	•	•
Astro Ventilation vent-ports	•	•
Electric clock	•	•
Automatic ignition key alarm	•	•
Glove compartment lock and light	•	•
Illuminated heater control panel	•	•
Cigarette lighter	•	•
Oil pressure, temperature, and generator warning light	•	•
Parking brake and brake system warning light	•	•
Soft turn signal and shift lever knobs	•	•
Padded instrument panel and sun visors	•	•

Monte Carlo Interior Features	Coupe	SS
Convenient T-handle parking brake release	•	•
Wide day-night rearview mirror	•	•
Foot-operated parking brake	•	•
Suspended accelerator pedal	•	•
Bright forward-mounted door lock buttons	•	•
Clear window regulator handles	•	•
Padded front door armrests with bright accents	•	•
Rear seat armrests with built-in ashtrays	•	•
Scuff-resistant plastic cowl side panels	•	•
Vinyl assist grips on doors	•	•
Extra-thick foam cushioned front and rear seats	•	•
Deep-twist carpeting on floor, lower door trim panel	•	•
Vinyl-coated perforated headlining	•	•
Center dome light with bright bezel	•	•
Vinyl-coated luggage compartment mat	•	•

Interior features of the 1971 Monte Carlo.

71

Exterior Dimensions	coupe
Wheelbase	116.0
Length (overall)	206.5
Width (overall)	75.6
Height (loaded)	52.9
Front tread	60.3
Rear tread	59.3

Interior Roominess	
Head room—front	37.6
Head room—rear	36.3
Leg room—front	42.8
Leg room—rear	32.3
Hip room—front	59.4
Hip room—rear	53.0
Shoulder room—front	58.0
Shoulder room—rear	56.6
Front entrance height	29.5

Luggage Compartment	coupe
Maximum opening width	48.5
Loading height	25.7
Interior length (max.)	49.0
Interior width (max.)	72.0
Interior height (max.)	18.0
Usable luggage space (cu. ft.)	12.9

Glass Area	
Windshield glass area (sq. in.)	1206.7
Rear window glass area (sq. in.)	1059.4
Total glass area (sq. in.)	3493.5

Tire Size & Steering Specifications	
Standard tire size	G78 x 15*
Turning circle—curb-to-curb (ft.)	42.0
Turning circle—wall-to-wall (ft.)	45.5
Steering ratio—std. (overall)	28.7:1
Steering ratio—power (overall)	18.7 to 12.4

Fuel Capacity & Weight	
Rated fuel tank capacity (gallons)	19
Curb weight—(lbs.)	3594
Shipping weight—(lbs.)	3496

*G70 x 15 white stripe tires and 15 x 7 wheels included with SS equipment.

Vinyl Roof Cover*Color Choices (RPO C08)

vinyl roof color	code	exterior color availability
Black	BB	all exterior colors
Dark Blue	CC	Tuxedo Black, Nevada Silver, Antique White, Ascot Blue or Malsanne Blue
Dark Brown	FF	Classic Copper, Burnt Orange, Rosewood Metallic, Sandalwood or Antique White
Dark Green	GG	Tuxedo Black, Lime Green, Cottonwood Green, Antique Green or Antique White
White	AA	all exterior colors

*Optional at extra cost.   Note: Roof and rear quarter belt molding inside surfaces match vinyl roof color.

Seat and Shoulder Belt Colors

interior trim color	standard belts	custom deluxe belts*
Black	Black	Black
Dark Blue	Black	Dark Blue
Dark Jade	Black	Dark Jade
Saddle	Black	Beige
Sandalwood	Black	Sandalwood

*Available at extra cost.   Note: Standard seat and shoulder belt buckles black; Custom Deluxe buckles brush-finished.

Specifications for 1971 models.

Engines, Transmissions and Axle Ratios

engines	transmissions and rear axle ratios			
	3-Speed (2.54:1 low)	4-Speed (2.52:1 low)	Powerglide	Turbo Hydra-matic
Standard V8	3.08		3.08	2.73 *
(RPO L48) 270-hp (175▲) Turbo-Fire 350 V8		3.31		2.73
(RPO LS3) 300-hp (260▲) Turbo-Jet 400 V8		3.31		2.73
365-hp (285▲) Turbo-Jet 454 V8 (Included with Monte Carlo SS RPO Z20)				3.31

▲SAE net (as installed) horsepower   *Trailering ratio: 3.31:1   Note: Positraction rear axle available in all axle ratios.

Equipment Included With Optional* V8 Engines

	270-hp (175▲) 350	300-hp (260▲) 400	365-hp (285▲) 454**
Special front and rear springs			•
Heavier duty shock absorbers		(rear only)	•
Rear axle ring gear—8.875" dia.		•	•
Single exhaust (2½-in. dia.)	•		
Dual exhaust (2½-in. dia.)		•	•
Larger capacity radiator		•	•
Heavier duty battery			•
15 x 7 Rally Wheels			•
Automatic Level Control			•
Heavier duty clutch	•	•	
Higher performance starting motor	•	•	•
Deep cover fuel pump and vapor return line to fuel tank		•	•
Heavier front stabilizer			•
Rear stabilizer			•

▲SAE net (as installed) horsepower   *Optional at extra cost. **Included with Monte Carlo SS equipment (RPO Z20).

Engine features for 1971.

CHAPTER NINE
High Style,
Easy Handling
And New Grilles For '72

Both Chevelle and Monte Carlo saw a few changes in their 1972 models. This small appearance difference was caused by a strike at General Motors in 1971 when plans were being made for a new design on the next year's cars. Therefore, the 1972 Chevelle appeared with a design going into its fifth year without any drastic changes; the Monte Carlo looked nearly the same for its third year.

Using the same body shell, Chevelle came with its two wheelbases for another year. The grille was enough changed to let you know that the car was a 1972. Also, the parking lights took on a new shape. The same number of models that was available in 1971 reappeared for 1972, the last season for this body style.

The factory was playing the same old song again about quality ride, easy handling and overall comfort. Actually, the ride was just the same as it had been for the previous years of these two cars.

Monte Carlo was now entering its third year of the "first generation." As stated earlier, little change was seen in this new model except for a wider grille and parking lights set between the grille and the new

Coming only as a V-8 was the Malibu convertible, which weighed 3,379 pounds. The manufacturers list price for the rag top void of any special trim was $3,186. By the time it got to the dealership with shipping preparations, taxes and so on the customer was looking at $3,550.

The 1972 Chevelle Malibu sport coupe was introduced to the public on September 23, 1971. This was the most popular model among Chevelle buyers for 1972. It weighed 3,327 pounds and sold for $3,286 with the 307 ci V-8 engine.

Power-Beam headlights. The Monte Carlo and Chevelle were introduced to the public on Thursday, September 23, 1971.

The Monte Carlo continued to offer a wide selection of accessories to make driving more enjoyable. Strangely, with all the goodies that were available during this three-year life span such as a tachometer and water temperature gauge, no oil gauge was ever offered as a Chevrolet option for either Chevelle or Monte Carlo. All dash controls for these cars were neatly and conveniently located.

The rear seating of a Monte Carlo can be extremely tight unless you are under five years old. I recall picking up my family in Canada when my beige Monte Carlo was practically new. It was pretty filled with various automobilia from a trip I took to Detroit. All this and four more people to sandwich into the car made me realize it wasn't a true family car but more of a personal luxury car meant for two adults and maybe a couple of children under five years of age.

The name Monte Carlo Custom appeared only in 1972. What made it different was left-hand remote-control sport mirror, belt molding, custom wheel covers, 15x7 wheels, G70x15 blackwall tires, custom steering wheel (four-spoke Sport steering wheel when Comfortilt was ordered), auxiliary lighting (ashtray light, courtesy floor lights, mirror map light, luggage compartment light and underhood light), Sport suspension with front and rear ride stabilizers, and a special acoustical package. These options were referred to as Z03, which added $213.45 to a Monte Carlo or, to put it another way, were classed as standard equipment if you purchased a Monte Carlo Custom. A vinyl roof cover and white-stripe tires could be ordered in place of the G70x15 blackwalls as extra cost items if the owner desired them.

The SS 454 was now on its way out the door. The California Emmissions Control law preventing the larger engines from being sold certainly did its part. Trying to hold on, though, Chevrolet still offered a Monte Carlo with options like bucket seats, Rally wheels and the detuned 454 engine developing 270 hp. The number of 1972 Monte Carlos produced is not currently available from Chevrolet.

Introduced in mid-season 1971 was this 1972 Heavy Chevy, Model 13437, equipped with black-accented grille. Special side striping; Heavy Chevy decal on hood, front fender and rear deck; special domed hood with locking pins; 14x6 rally-type wheels with special trim were included in a package which cost $138 in addition to the base price of $3,286.

A 1972 SS sport coupe with all its "bomb equipment" brought an additional $350 to the special coupe. This same package was available on the convertible, too.

One last remark about the Monte Carlos of this three-year period is that they were always in big demand when new. Rarely did one ever go out the door for which a customer didn't pay full sticker price or darn close to it.

The cars of this nine-year span are becoming more valuable all the time. Take care of your "pride and joy" as it can only appreciate in the years ahead.

Chevelle's most-expensive vehicle for 1972 came as the Concours estate wagon once again. It weighed 2,775 pounds and sold for $3,901 if it was an eight-passenger model. The six-passenger version was about 100 pounds less and sold for approximately $100 less.

Practical Chevelle and Heavy Chevy models came with long-wearing cloth seating, vinyl door and seat ends for easy maintenance.

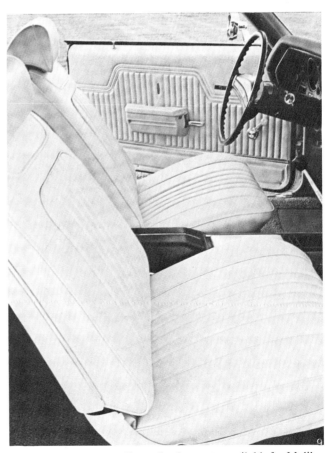

Sporty buckets were available for Malibu sport coupes and convertibles. This trim equipment made the inside look as sporty as the racing decals on the outside.

SS Convertible

A true muscle-car sits here. It's the '72 SS convertible "just a-rarin' to go."

A new front end for Monte Carlo. This personal luxury car was virtually unchanged except for the wider grille and parking lights. This model weighed 3,506 pounds and had a base price of $3,225. Very, very few ever left the factory at that price. Most people who ordered this unit usually went pretty much with the full package of options.

Seen here is the 1972 Monte Carlo, minus the fender skirts. By 1972 the price of the skirts was $16.50 when ordered with the car.

This Monte Carlo sports fender skirts.

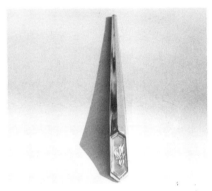

The simple hood ornament used on the 1972 Monte Carlo resembled the 1970 models more than the 1971 cars. M. C. was inscribed at the base of the ornament.

Solid comfort is what the seats of this 1972 Monte Carlo had to offer. They were available in either cloth or vinyl.

Wider grille bars and the vertical parking lamps mounted between the grille and the headlamps were the only major change seen on the 1972 Monte Carlo.

SEDANS, COUPES & CONVERTIBLE
1972 MODELS WITH STANDARD EQUIPMENT

Model		List Price	Factory D&H	Mfr's Sgt'd Retail★	Dest'n Charge	Total
6-CYLINDER MODELS						
Chevelle						
13337	Sport Coupe	$2657.00	$ 11.70	$2668.70	————	————
13369	4-Door Sedan	2624.00	11.70	2635.70	————	————
Malibu						
13537	Sport Coupe	2821.00	11.70	2832.70	————	————
13569	4-Door Sedan	2789.00	11.70	2800.70	————	————
V8 MODELS						
Chevelle						
13437	Sport Coupe	2747.00	11.70	2758.70	————	————
13469	4-Door Sedan	2714.00	11.70	2725.70	————	————
Malibu						
13637	Sport Coupe	2911.00	11.70	2922.70	————	————
13669	4-Door Sedan	2879.00	11.70	2890.70	————	————
13639	Sport Sedan	2979.00	11.70	2990.70	————	————
13667	Convertible	3175.00	11.70	3186.70	————	————

★Does not include state and local taxes, license fees, options or accessories.

STANDARD EQUIPMENT

Air Cleaner: Oil-wetted paper

Axle, Front: Independent suspension; coil springs; stabilizer bar

Axle, Rear: Semi-floating housing; four-link type suspension; coil springs; ratio, 3.08

Battery: 12-volt; 6-cyl—45-amp-hr V8—61-amp-hr

Belts, Seat: All passenger positions

Belts, Shoulder: Driver and RH passenger (front) (except Convertible)

Brakes, Service: Hydraulic; self-adjusting; dual system; drum and shoe type
Front: size 9.5" x 2.5"
Rear: size 9.5" x 2.0"
Total effective lining area: 151.6 sq in

Brakes, Parking: Rear wheels

Clutch: 6-cyl—Dia. 9.12", 71.82 sq in V8—Dia. 10.34", 101.54 sq in

Cooling: 1.26" core; cross-flow type; effective area 353 sq in

Engines: 6-Cyl—110-hp 250 cu in V8—130-hp 307 cu in

Emission Control Equipment

Frame: Welded, perimeter type

Fuel Tank: Capacity approx. 19 gallons

Generator: 37-amp Delcotron

Head Restraints: Front, driver and RH passenger

Heater and Defroster

Oil Filter: Full-flow; 1 pt; throwaway type

Shock Absorbers: Front and rear

Tires: Five E78-14B bias belted ply blackwall

Transmission: Fully synchronized 3-speed; steering column shift lever

Wheels: 14" x 5"

Windshield Washer and Wipers: Electric, 2-speed

POPULAR OPTIONAL EQUIPMENT◆

Description	Opt No.	List Price	Factory D&H	Mfr's Sgt'd Retail Delv'rd◆
MODEL OPTIONS				
SS Equipment: V8 Malibu Sport Coupe or Convertible models with optional engine and transmission only. Includes power disc/drum brakes; black-finished grille; special domed hood with locking pins; LH remote-controlled sport mirror; SS emblem on grille, fenders and steering wheel; 15" x 7" wheels with special trim; F60-15 white lettered tires and sport suspension	Z15	$347.00	$3.05	$350.05
Heavy Chevy: Model 13437 V8 Chevelle Sport Coupe only. Includes black-accented grille; special side striping; Heavy Chevy decals on hood, front fenders and rear deck; special domed hood with locking pins; 14" x 6" rally type wheels with special trim.				
With black striping	YF3/YF8	138.00	—	138.00
With white striping	YF3/ZR8	138.00	—	138.00

Features of the 1972 Chevelle.

Description	Opt No.	List Price	Factory D&H	Mfr's Sgst'd Retail Delvr'd

FEATURE GROUPS*

Description	Opt No.	List Price	Factory D&H	Mfr's Sgst'd Retail Delvr'd
Appearance Guard Group—Includes:				
(A) **Front and Rear Bumper Guards**	V30	$ 31.00	—	$ 31.00
(B) **Door Edge Guards**—2-Door models	B93	6.00	—	6.00
4-Door models	B93	9.00	—	9.00
(C) **Color-Keyed Floor Mats**—2 front and 2 rear (All models)	B37	12.00	—	12.00
(D) **Vanity Visor Mirror**	D34	3.00	—	3.00
All 2-door models — Includes A, B, C & D	ZP5	52.00	—	52.00
All 4-door models — Includes A, B, C & D	ZP5	55.00	—	55.00
Operating Convenience Group—Includes:				
(A) **Electric Clock** (Included in Special Instrumentation option)	U35	16.00	—	16.00
(B) **Rear Window Defroster:** Forced Air Coupes and Sedans	C50	31.00	—	31.00
Convertible	C50	36.00	—	36.00
(C) **Outside LH Remote-Control Rearview Mirror** (All models)	D33	12.00	—	12.00
For Malibu Sedans—Include A, B & C	ZQ2	59.00	—	59.00
Coupes without SS Equipment:				
Without special instrumentation—Incl A, B & C	ZQ2	59.00	—	59.00
With special instrumentation—Incl B & C	ZQ2	43.00	—	43.00
Coupes with SS Equipment:				
Without special instrumentation—Incl A & B	ZQ2	47.00	—	47.00
With special instrumentation—Incl B	ZQ2	31.00	—	31.00
Convertible without SS Equipment:				
Without special instrumentation—Incl A, B & C	ZQ2	64.00	—	64.00
With special instrumentation—Incl C	ZQ2	12.00	—	12.00
Convertible with SS Equipment:				
Without special instrumentation—Incl B	ZQ2	36.00	—	36.00
For Chevelle Sedan—Incl A, B & C	ZQ2	59.00	—	59.00
Sport Coupe:				
Without special instrumentation—Incl A, B & C	ZQ2	59.00	—	59.00
With special instrumentation—Incl B & C	ZQ2	43.00	—	43.00

Any item contained in Feature Groups may be ordered separately.

POWER TEAMS

Description	Opt No.	List Price	Factory D&H	Mfr's Sgst'd Retail Delvr'd
Engines: V8 models only				
†165-hp Turbo-Fire 350 V8	L65	26.00		26.00
†175-hp Turbo-Fire 350 V8	L48	72.00		72.00
††240-hp Turbo-Jet 400 V8 (requires F78-14 tires)	LS3	168.00		168.00
††270-hp Turbo-Jet 454 V8 (requires SS Equipment and HD battery)	LS5	272.00		272.00
Transmissions:				
Powerglide—with standard engines only				
6-cyl models	M35	174.00		174.00
V8 models	M35	185.00		185.00
Turbo Hydra-matic—V8 models only				
With standard, 165-hp or 175-hp engine	M40	210.00		210.00
With 240-hp or 270-hp engine	M40	231.00		231.00
3-Speed. Floor mounted (w/165-hp or 175-hp V8 only)	M11	128.00		128.00
Special 3-Speed. Floor mounted (w/240-hp V8 only)	MC1	128.00		128.00
4-Speed Wide Range. Requires console (w/240-hp V8 only)	M20	190.00		190.00
Special 4-Speed Close Ratio (w/270-hp V8 only)	M22	231.00		231.00

† Available for registration in the State of California
†† Not available for registration in the State of California

Description	Opt No.	List Price	Factory D&H	Mfr's Sgst'd Retail Delvr'd
Axle, Positraction Rear	G80	$ 45.00	—	$ 45.00
Axle Ratios: Requires Turbo Hydra-matic				
Trailering—Requires special suspension and V8 engine (not avail. w/270-hp)	YD1	12.00	—	12.00
Performance—with standard V8 only	ZQ9	12.00	—	12.00

POWER ASSISTS

Description	Opt No.	List Price	Factory D&H	Mfr's Sgst'd Retail Delvr'd
Brakes, Power:				
With drum-type brakes	J50	46.00		46.00
With disc/drum brakes. Included with SS Equipment	JL2	68.00		68.00
Door Locks, Power: 2-door models	AU3	45.00		45.00
4-door models	AU3	69.00		69.00
Steering, Power: Variable ratio	N40	113.00		113.00

OTHER OPTIONS

Description	Opt No.	List Price	Factory D&H	Mfr's Sgst'd Retail Delvr'd
Air Conditioning, Four-Season: Includes 61-amp Delcotron and increased cooling V8 models only	C60	397.00	—	397.00
Battery, Heavy-Duty: 80-ampere-hour	T60	15.00		15.00
Belts, Custom Deluxe Seat and Shoulder: *REPLACING STANDARD NUMBER OF BELTS--*				
Coupes with Bucket seats—5 seat & 2 front shoulder	AK1	14.50		14.50
Coupes and Sedans with Bench seats—6 seat & 2 front shoulder	AK1	16.00		16.00
Convertible with Bucket seats—5 seat	A39	12.50		12.50
Convertible with Bench seat—6 seat	A39	14.00		14.00
SHOULDER BELTS ONLY--				
Convertible (requires Custom Deluxe seat belts) 2 Front	A85	26.00		26.00
California Assembly Line Emission Test: Released to conform with State of California registration requirements. Not available on standard, 240-hp or 270-hp V8 engines	YF5	15.00		15.00

Description	Opt No.	List Price	Factory D&H	Mfr's Sgst'd Retail Delvr'd
Console: Malibu Sport Coupe or Convertible models only. Requires bucket seats and optional transmission	D55	57.00	—	57.00
Generator, 63-Amp Delcotron:				
Without air conditioning	K85	26.00	—	26.00
With air conditioning	K85	5.00	—	5.00
Glass, Soft-Ray Tinted: All windows	A01	42.00	—	42.00
Hood, Cowl Induction: Available with 240- or 270-hp V8 and SS Equipment only. Includes sport striping on hood and rear deck lid, air intake valve at rear of hood and hood to air cleaner duct.				
With black striping	ZL2/YF8	154.00	—	154.00
With white striping. (Not available with white exterior paint)	ZL2/ZR8	154.00	—	154.00
Instrumentation, Special: Available on V8 Coupes and Convertibles only. Includes electric clock, tachometer, ammeter and temperature gauges	U14	82.00	—	82.00
Lighting, Auxiliary—Includes: (A) Ashtray Light (B) Courtesy Lights (C) Glove Compartment Light (D) Luggage Compartment Light (E) Mirror Map Light (F) Underhood Light				
Convertible—Includes A, D, E & F	ZJ9	$ 15.00	—	$ 15.00
Malibu Coupes and Sedans—Includes A, B, D, E & F	ZJ9	21.00	—	21.00
Chevelle Coupes and Sedans—Includes A, B, C, D, E & F	ZJ9	23.50	—	23.50
Moldings:				
Window. 4-Door Sedans only	B90	26.00	—	26.00
Body Side	B84	33.00	—	33.00
Paint, Exterior:				
Solid		N.C.	—	N.C.
Two-tone. Includes bright outline moldings		31.00	—	31.00
Radiator, Heavy-Duty:				
6-Cyl models	V01	14.00	—	14.00
V8 models—Includes extra HD Cooling	V01	21.00	—	21.00
Radio Equipment:				
Radios, Pushbutton—				
AM Radio	U63	65.00	—	65.00
AM/FM Radio	U69	135.00	—	135.00
AM/FM/Stereo Radio	U79	233.00	—	233.00
Speaker, Rear Seat—Not available when Stereo is ordered	U80	15.00	—	15.00
Stereo Tape System—				
With AM Radio	UM1	195.00	—	195.00
With AM/FM/Stereo Radio	UM2	363.00	—	363.00
Roof Cover, Vinyl: Includes bright outline moldings				
Black	BB	92.00	—	92.00
Blue (Medium) w/black moldings	DD	*See Chevrolet Price*		
Pewter, Silver. w/black moldings	HH	*Schedule for Availability*		
Covert (Light)	TT	92.00	—	92.00
Green (Medium)	GG	92.00	—	92.00
Tan (Medium)	FF	92.00	—	92.00
White	AA	92.00	—	92.00
Seats:				
Strato-Bucket Vinyl Malibu Sport Coupe or convertible only	A51	133.00	—	133.00
Vinyl Bench Coupes or Sedans only		18.00	—	18.00
Speed and Cruise Control: (Cruise-Master). For V8 models with automatic transmission and power brakes	K30	62.00	—	62.00
Steering Wheels:				
Comfortilt; requires optional transmission	N33	44.00	—	44.00
Custom	NK2	15.00	—	15.00
Sport; (4-spoke)	NK4	15.00	—	15.00
Stripes, Sport: Malibu Coupe or Convertible only. Included with cowl induction hood.				
Black	D88/YF8	77.00	—	77.00
White	D88/ZR8	77.00	—	77.00
Suspension, Special Front and Rear: Includes special springs and shock absorbers. Not available with SS Equipment	F40	17.00	—	17.00
Suspension, Sport: Available only with 240-hp engine. Includes HD rear shock absorbers, front and rear springs, special front and rear stabilizers, and rear axle control arms. Included with SS Equipment	F41	30.00	—	30.00
Top, Convertible: Power				
White	AA	N.C.	—	N.C.
Black	BB	N.C.	—	N.C.
Wheel Covers: Not available with Heavy Chevy or SS Equipment				
Bright Metal	P01	$ 26.00	—	$ 26.00
Custom	P02	82.00	—	82.00
Wheels, Rally: Includes special 14' x 6" wheels, hub caps and trim rings. Not available with Heavy Chevy or SS Equipment	ZJ7	44.00	—	44.00

OPTIONAL TUBELESS TIRES—Factory Installed

Replacing (5) E78-14 B Bias Belted Ply Blackwall (without SS Equipment)

Description	Opt No.	List Price	Factory D&H	Mfr's Sgst'd Retail Delvr'd
(5) E78-14/B Bias Belted Ply White Stripe	PL3	28.00	N.C.	28.00
(5) F78-14/B Bias Belted Ply Blackwall Without 240-hp engine	PX5	16.50	$ .90	17.40
With 240-hp engine; Includes 14' x 6" wheels	PX5	22.50	.90	23.40
(5) F78-14/B Bias Belted Ply White Stripe Without 240-hp engine	PX6	46.50	.90	47.40
With 240-hp engine; Includes 14' x 6" wheels	PX6	51.50	.90	52.40

♦Popular Chevrolet installed options. See latest Chevrolet Price Schedule or Truck Data Book for complete list of optional equipment.   ♦State and local taxes not included

PLEASE NOTE: *The exterior and interior combinations for solid color paint shown in the chart below have been established as the combinations that would be attractive to the average customer. Orders for non-recommended solid color exterior and interior trim combinations may be submitted, provided the dealer initials the appropriate order form block as verification that the requested combination is definitely desired.*

This procedure does not apply to orders that specify a vinyl roof cover, or two-tone paint as combinations shown are the only combinations that have been approved.

VINYL ROOF		SOLID EXTERIOR COLOR AVAILABILITY
BLACK	BB	All Exterior Colors.
BLUE (Medium)	DD	White or Ascot Blue Exterior Colors only.
COVERT (Light)	TT	Bronze, Brown, Gold, Sequoia Green, Orange, Tan, White or Yellow Exterior Colors only.
GREEN (Medium)	GG	Gulf or Sequoia Green, Silver or White Exterior Colors only.
PEWTER, SILVER	HH	White, Silver or Sequoia Green Exterior Colors only.
TAN (Medium)	FF	Bronze, Mohave Gold or White Exterior Colors only.
WHITE	AA	All Exterior Colors.

INTERIOR TRIM & COLOR CODE

	Type of Seat	Black Cloth	Black Vinyl	Blue (Dark) Cloth	Covert (Light) Cloth	Covert (Light) Vinyl	Green (Dark) Cloth	Green (Dark) Vinyl	Pewter (Medium) Cloth	Saddle (Dark) Vinyl
COUPE	Bench	706	708	725	731	734	715		740	735
	Strato-Bucket (Opt. A51)	706	708					717	740	735

EXTERIOR COLOR	Lower Code	Upper Code	Black Cloth	Black Vinyl	Blue (Dark) Cloth	Covert Cloth	Covert Vinyl	Green Cloth	Green Vinyl	Pewter Cloth	Saddle Vinyl
SOLID											
Blue, Ascot	24	24	X		X						
Blue, Mulsanne	26	26	X		X						
Bronze, Midnight	68	68	X			X					X
Brown, Golden	57	57	X			X					
Gold, Mohave	63	63	X			X					X
Gold, Placer	53	53	X			X					X
Green, Gulf	43	43	X			X		X			
Green, Sequoia	48	48	X			X		X			X
Green, Spring	36	36	X								X
Orange, Flame	65	65	X								X
Red, Cranberry	75	75	X								X
Silver, Pewter	14	14	X					X		X	X
Tan, Covert	50	50	X			X		X			X
White, Antique	11	11	X		X	X		X		X	X
Yellow, Cream	56	56	X			X					X
TWO-TONE (With Antique White Upper Only)	Lower	Upper									
Blue, Mulsanne (Lower)	26	11	X		X						
Brown, Golden (Lower)	57	11	X			X					
Gold, Mohave (Lower)	63	11	X			X					X
Green, Gulf (Lower)	43	11	X			X		X			
Green, Sequoia (Lower)	48	11	X			X		X			X

POWER TEAMS

Transmission	Opt No.	Engine Usage
3-Speed Full Synchro	Std	165-hp V8
Powerglide	M35	165-hp V8
Turbo Hydra-matic	M40	165-hp V8 175-hp V8 240-hp V8 270-hp V8

SPECIFICATIONS

Wheelbase		116.0
Length (overall)		206.5
Width (overall)		75.6
Height (loaded)		52.9
Tread: Front		60.3
Rear		59.3
Interior Room:	FRONT	REAR
Head Room	37.6	36.3
Leg Room	42.8	32.3
Hip Room	59.4	53.0
Shoulder Room	58.0	56.6
Entrance Height	29.5	....
Luggage Space (cu. ft.): Usable		12.9
Tire Size		G78–15/B
Turning Diameter (feet): Curb-to-curb		42.0
Wall-to-Wall		45.5
Steering Ratio (overall): Standard Power		18.5:1 to 12.4:1
Curb Weight (lbs)		3603

Features of the 1972 Monte Carlo.

MONTE CARLO

Description	Opt No.	List Price	Factory D&H	Mfr's Sgt'd Retail Delvr'd♦
POWER TEAMS				
Engines: Available with Turbo Hydra-matic only				
175-hp Turbo-Fire 350 V8. Available for registration in the State of California	L48	$ 46.00	—	$ 46.00
240-hp Turbo-Jet 400 V8. Not available for registration in the State of California	LS3	142.00	—	142.00
270-hp Turbo-Jet 454 V8. Requires HD battery. Not available for registration in the State of California	LS5	261.00	—	261.00
Transmissions:				
Powerglide (with standard engine only)	M35	185.00	—	185.00
Turbo Hydra-matic—				
With standard or 175-hp V8	M40	210.00	—	210.00
With 240-hp or 270-hp V8	M40	231.00	—	231.00
Axle, Positraction Rear:	G80	45.00	—	45.00
Axle Ratio:				
Trailering — with standard engine and Turbo Hydra-matic only	YD1	12.00	—	12.00
POWER ASSISTS				
Door Lock System, Power	AU3	45.00	—	45.00
Seat, Power: Electric; 4-way				
With bench seat	A41	77.00	—	77.00
With bucket seats; driver's seat only	A46	77.00	—	77.00
Windows, Power	A31	124.00	—	124.00
OTHER OPTIONS				
Air Conditioning, Four-Season: Includes 61-amp Delcotron and increased cooling	C60	397.00	—	397.00
Battery, Heavy-Duty: 80-ampere-hour	T60	15.00	—	15.00
Belts, Custom Deluxe Seat and Shoulder: REPLACING STANDARD NUMBER OF BELTS—				
Coupes with Bucket seats—5 seat & 2 front shoulder	AK1	16.00	—	16.00
Coupes with Bench seats—6 seat & 2 front shoulder	AK1	14.50	—	14.50
California Assembly Line Emission Test: Released to conform with State of California registration requirements. Not available on 240-hp or 270-hp engines	YF5	15.00	—	15.00
Console: Requires bucket seats. Not available with standard transmission	D55	57.00	—	57.00
Generator, 63-amp Delcotron:				
With air conditioning	K85	5.00	—	5.00
Without air conditioning	K85	26.00	—	26.00
Glass, Soft-Ray Tinted: All windows	A01	45.00	—	45.00
Instrumentation, Special: Includes tachometer, ammeter and temperature gauges	U14	67.00	—	67.00
Lighting, Auxiliary: Includes ashtray, courtesy, luggage compartment, mirror map and underhood lights	Z19	21.00	—	21.00
Moldings, Belt	B85	18.00	—	18.00
Paint Exterior:				
Solid		N.C.	—	N.C.
Two-tone		51.00	—	51.00
Radiator, Heavy-Duty: Included when 270-hp engine with air conditioning is ordered	V01	21.00	—	21.00
Radio Equipment:				
Radios, Pushbutton				
AM Radio	U63	65.00	—	65.00
AM/FM Radio	U69	135.00	—	135.00
AM/FM/Stereo Radio	U79	233.00	—	233.00

Description	Opt No.	List Price	Factory D&H	Mfr's Sgt'd Retail Delvr'd♦
OTHER OPTIONS (cont'd)				
Radio Equipment (Cont'd):				
Speaker, Rear Seat—Not available when Stereo is ordered	U80	$ 15.00	—	$ 15.00
Stereo Tape System				
With AM Radio	UM1	195.00	—	195.00
With AM/FM/Stereo Radio	UM2	363.00	—	363.00
Roof Cover, Vinyl: Includes bright outline moldings—Black	BB	123.00	—	123.00
Blue (Medium) w/black moldings	DD	*See Chevrolet Price*		
Pewter, Silver, w/black moldings	HH	*Schedule for Availability*		
Covert (Light)	TT	123.00	—	123.00
Green (Medium)	GG	123.00	—	123.00
Tan (Medium)	FF	123.00	—	123.00
White	AA	123.00	—	123.00
Seats: Strato-Bucket, cloth or vinyl	A51	133.00	—	133.00
Vinyl Bench Seat		18.00	—	18.00
Shock Absorber, Rear: Superlift automatic level control	G67	87.00	—	87.00
Skirts, Rear Fender: Not available with 15' x 7' wheels or custom wheel covers	T58	31.00	—	31.00
Speed and Cruise Control: (Cruise-Master) Available only with automatic transmission. Not available with superlift rear shocks	K30	62.00	—	62.00
Steering Wheels:				
Comfortilt; requires optional transmission	N33	44.00	—	44.00
Custom	NK2	15.00	—	15.00
Sport; (4-spoke)	NK4	15.00	—	15.00
Wheel Covers:				
Deluxe	PA3	15.00	—	15.00
Custom. Includes 15' x 7' wheels	PO2	78.00	—	78.00
Wheels, 15' x 7': Included with Monte Carlo Custom and custom wheel covers	PH1	10.00	—	10.00
Wheels, Rally: Not available with Monte Carlo Custom. Includes special 15' x 7' wheels, hub caps and trim rings	ZJ7	40.00	—	40.00
OPTIONAL TUBELESS TIRES—Factory Installed				
Replaces (5) G78-15/B Bias Belted Ply Blackwall				
(5) G78-15/B Bias Belted Ply White Stripe. Not available with Monte Carlo Custom	PU8	32.00	N.C.	32.00
(5) G70-15/B Bias Belted Ply White Stripe. Without Monte Carlo Custom. Requires 15' x 7' wheels, rally wheels or custom wheel covers	P90	48.00	.45	48.45
With Monte Carlo Custom	P90	30.00	N.C.	30.00

♦ Popular Chevrolet installed options. See latest Chevrolet Price Schedule or Truck Data Book for complete list of optional equipment. ♦State and local taxes not included.